INTERSTATE RELATIONS
IN AUSTRALIA

Richard H. Leach

INTERSTATE RELATIONS
IN AUSTRALIA

University of Kentucky Press

TO

QUEENIE

who reigns supreme

PREFACE

This study grew out of a continuing interest in cooperation
among the units of federal systems that I first felt as a
member of the staff of the Southern Regional Education
Board, itself an interstate agency devoted to the development
of higher education in the South through cooperative programs among Southern universities. A study of interstate
cooperation in the United States I began there culminated in
a book written with Redding S. Sugg, Jr., *The Administration
of Interstate Compacts*, published in 1959, and in a number
of shorter pieces published since 1957 in several scholarly and
professional journals. I turned next to Canada and to inter-
provincial relations there, and the results of that study were
summarized in an article in *Canadian Public Administration*
in 1959. During the 1956-1957 academic year, Professor K. C.
Wheare was in residence at Duke. He first suggested the
possibility of extending my study to his native Australia. But
it was not until later, in the winter of 1959-1960, when
Professor P. H. Partridge of the Australian National University in Canberra was at Duke, that the idea began to take
form. Professor Partridge agreed with Professor Wheare's
conclusion that interstate cooperation had been neglected by
students of government in Australia, and he urged me to
undertake to fill the gap. With his help, I developed a list of
state officials in every state, to all of whom I subsequently
wrote, laying out the general scheme of the project and asking
their assistance. The response was remarkable. Every one
of them assured me heartily of both the need for a study of
interstate relations in Australia and his willingness to assist
me in making it. The remark of the Victorian Minister of

Education, John Bloomfield, was typical of the comments I received: "Your letter has started a stream of thought on this subject which may well produce some beneficial results as far as the satisfactory working of the Federal system is concerned."

The problem then was to collect my basic data. There were no published studies of interstate relations to draw upon. And although the premiers of three states—New South Wales, Victoria, and Queensland—had in response to my letter circulated every department in their state governments for information on their relations with departments in other states and had supplied me with copies of every report submitted to them, and though a great many state officials in the other three states had replied in some detail to my letter, all of which was very helpful to me, by and large Australian state government officials had not articulated the degree and the variety of interstate activities many of them were actually engaged in. My only recourse was thus to go to Australia and see interstate cooperation in action, in part through study of state department and agency papers and reports, available only in departmental files, but chiefly through personal interviews with state premiers, department heads, and civil servants, the people who were themselves in the midst of interstate activities and programs. Fortunately, it was time for a sabbatical leave from my duties at Duke, and the Department of Political Science, through its Ford Grant for Public Affairs, and the University Council on Research were willing to subsidize a trip "down under." I left in June 1961 and was in Australia until the end of the year. I found everyone I contacted there as hospitable as anyone could be. Without the generous assistance of innumerable state officials (most of whom unfortunately asked me not to use their names) I would not have been able to carry out my project at all. I wish that I could list them all by name, for I still remember their unfailing kindness, and I would like to thank them formally for all their efforts on my behalf.

Whether I have done justice to the data I collected through their kind intercession remains for the reader to determine. I realize that this study is only a beginning, in that it is concerned chiefly with interstate relations as they now exist in Australia and thus does not deal to any extent with their history. With Professor John Ward of the University of Sydney, I agree that there is real need for a historical study to be undertaken. Moreover, this study is necessarily descriptive in nature. Until I began work in the field, the status of Australian interstate relations was virtually unknown. The first thing that had to be done was to uncover and describe them. This is basically all I have tried to do. Now that the facts about interstate relations are available, criticism and analysis can follow. Furthermore, I have limited myself to official relations between state governments. I have not dealt with other interstate relations, such as those between labor unions, chambers of commerce, banks and insurance companies, down through a long list of nongovernmental groups and organizations. These too are areas that ought to be explored. I realize, finally, that interstate relations and Commonwealth-state relations are very much intertwined in Australia, even more than they are in the United States and Canada, and that to some extent an attempt to pull interstate relations out by themselves and look at them alone may subject them to possible distortion. I hope that this has not happened.

Most of the data on which this study is based was gathered during my visit in 1961. Subsequently I have brought a number of references up to date through mid-1964, but because of the general lack of published material on interstate relations in Australia, it has not been possible to keep track of every development in the field.

The completion of this project does not exhaust my interest in the general subject. I hope to broaden and deepen my knowledge of the three sister systems I have studied so far and eventually to pursue the subject in still other federal

systems. I would also like sometime to pay some attention
to the implications for political theory that arise from the
development of interstate relations in federal systems. The
whole subject of federalism is just now of great interest to
the world's developing nations. Perhaps some of the experiences of the older federal systems in solving some of their
problems through interstate cooperation will be of interest
to the newer nations as they set about to tackle their problems. It is my hope that my book might have some value in
that connection.

In conclusion, I would like to single out a few Australians
who went far beyond the call of Australian-American solidarity
in making my visit productive: Reginald McAllister, Premier's
Department, Queensland; T. H. Kewley and Peter Loveday,
Department of Government and Public Administration,
University of Sydney; P. H. Partridge and R. Gavin Boyd,
Australian National University; Sir Kenneth H. Bailey, Com-
monwealth Solicitor-General; Sir John Jungwirth, Premier's
Department, Victoria; W. A. Townsley, Department of Po-
litical Science, University of Tasmania; John Driscoll, Crown
Solicitor, Tasmania; Sir Thomas Playford, Premier, South
Australia; W. G. K. Duncan, Department of Political Science,
University of Adelaide; and Sir Alexander Reid, Chancellor,
and Fred Alexander, Department of History, University of
Western Australia. Although I have said thanks to each of
them personally, I want to do so publicly now.

Some of the material in Chapter 6 has appeared in different
form in the Spring 1963 issue of the *American Journal of
Comparative Law*.

My wife and son have been patient all during the time I
have been working on this book, and for that, as for so many
other things, I am grateful to them.

Myrtle Beach, South Carolina   Richard H. Leach
May 4, 1964

CONTENTS

Chapter 1 THE CONTEXT OF
INTERSTATE RELATIONS:
STATE DIFFERENCES

Probably no nation has undergone quite such tremendous
change and rapid development since its founding as has
Australia. Federation did not become a popular movement
until the midnineties, and the six Australian colonies did not
agree "to unite in one indissoluble Federal Commonwealth"
until 1900.[1] The Commonwealth itself did not come into
existence until January 1, 1901. Yet in the short space of a
mere sixty years, Australia has moved from a relatively
undeveloped agrarian society to a complex, highly industrial-
ized society and from the backwaters of world importance
and influence to a key position in the English-speaking world.
These changes have inevitably been reflected in Australian
government and particularly in the nature of her federal
system.

The Australian Constitution, like the United States and
Canadian constitutions, did not lay down specific instructions
to be followed in adapting the federal structure to changing
conditions, even though federation was from the first regarded
"not as a stage, but as something permanent."[2] Thus the
Constitution has been less meaningful than judicial interpretation and the pressure of economic forces in directing the
modification of Australian federalism. As the federation was
originally conceived, the states were to possess the residue of
power remaining after the Commonwealth government had
been granted power in such areas as defense, external affairs,
currency, immigration, and customs and excise. Indeed, the

states looked forward in 1901 to governing "largely as before
—looking after development, land policy and agriculture,
labour relations, education, health and social welfare"—the
really important subjects of government action—"having merely
shed to a convenient joint subsidiary certain common chores
of a less continually lively nature."[3] And for a long time their
expectations were borne out in practice. Even in 1930, it was
still true that: "The average citizen looks more frequently to
the Government which sits in Melbourne or Adelaide than
to the Government which sits in Canberra. It is this close,
more intimate Government which protects him from the
wicked, educates him, watches over his health, develops roads
and railways and water supplies . . . regulates his local trade
conditions, inspects his factory—performs, in short, all those
functions which seem to affect most nearly his economic and
social well-being."[4]

Time, however, was to play a trick on the states. The rapid
growth of population after federation, the development of
industry and commerce, and the birth of the welfare state all
created new problems that required new controls. These
pressures for alteration in the balance of federal power were
considerably strengthened by the two world wars and the
depression of 1929, all within a scant generation. The combination of all these factors resulted in a vast growth in
Commonwealth power, a growth which has been phenomenal
measured either by its financial resources or by its expanded
services.[5] Within forty years of federation, most Australians
had come to look to the Commonwealth rather than to the

[1] The phrase is from the preamble to the Commonwealth of Australia
Constitution Act, 63 and 64 Victoria, Chapter XII (1900).

[2] Gordon Greenwood, *The Future of Australian Federalism* (Melbourne,
1946), p. 35; see also Greenwood's comment on p. 37.

[3] A. F. Davies, "Victorian Government and Politics," in G. W. Leeper
(ed.), *Introducing Victoria* (Melbourne, 1955), p. 287.

[4] W. K. Hancock, *Australia* (New York, 1930), p. 76.

[5] A. J. Davies, "Federal Relations," in R. N. Spann (ed.), *Public Administration in Australia* (Sydney, n. d.), p. 60. The section, entitled "Changing Needs," of Davies' chapter is well worth reading in this connection.

states for their social and economic welfare.[6] The issues of federal politics and the programs of federal agencies had assumed much greater importance than they had had originally, while those of the states had somehow become "miscellaneous and mysterious."[7]

Federalism after the War

As the nation began to plan for its postwar development, it began to seem to some that further and possibly complete centralization was the only proper course. Prime Minister Chifley led those who held that point of view, demanding drastic amendment of the Constitution in response to what he described as the "need for a wider national outlook and greater Federal control of matters which [affect] the nation as a whole." "We must," he declared, "picture and hope for far wider powers for the Federal Parliament after the war."[8]

The Australian people, however, did not agree with Chifley. Whether because they had come to believe profoundly in federalism, or because "they thought the Federal Government was well occupied looking after defense, communications and customs, and such obviously Commonwealth affairs,"[9] or because of their own inertia, combined with the pressures of "vested interests and the genuine attachment to federalism of minority groups," they decided in no uncertain terms that the federal system must prevail, and that only details would be changed.[10] Not only did they reject all but one of the many proposals Chifley's Labour Party made to strengthen national

[6] P. H. Partridge, "Political Institutions and Aspirations," in George Caiger (ed.), *The Australian Way of Life* (New York, 1953), p. 71.
[7] Davies, "Victorian Government and Politics," p. 286.
[8] J. P. Chifley, "Reconstruction after the War," *Public Administration*, III (September 1941), 104. (This and subsequent references to this periodical are to volumes in its new series.)
[9] An alternative suggested by Colin Wills in his *Australian Passport* (New York, 1953), p. 107.
[10] "Amending the Constitution," *Current Affairs Bulletin*, XIX (February 25, 1957), 134.

power by amending the Constitution,[11] they subsequently turned Chifley and the Labour Party out of office as well.

In the campaign of 1949, the issue was clearly before the people. In the Joint Opposition Policy Statement with which Mr. Menzies opened the campaign, the question of federalism was given first place: "We continue to stand for the federal principle, that is, for a division of powers between Commonwealth and States, as distinct from complete centralisation of power at Canberra. We believe that government is most efficiently conducted when Commonwealth, States, and municipalities operate in their own spheres under the control of their own electors. . . . As we believe in the division of power, so we believe that the States must be preserved as real governing bodies and not as the mere dependents of the Commonwealth."

Although other issues were of course involved in the election, the assumption seems to be warranted that a majority of the Australian people agreed with the policy statement and accepted its premises, for the Liberal-Country coalition was victorious and has remained in office ever since. When a new party, the Commonwealth Centre Party, established just prior to the 1961 elections, included as a part of its twenty-point program a statement calling for the creation "of a single parliament for the whole of Australia with abolition of state parliaments,"[12] it failed conspicuously at the polls, not winning a single seat anywhere in the Commonwealth. The Australian people seem to be committed to federalism; by now, there is virtually no popular enthusiasm for further centralization.[13] The attitude of Sir Thomas Playford, long-

[11] See Commonwealth of Australia, *Convention of Representatives of the Commonwealth and State Parliaments on Proposed Alteration of the Commonwealth Constitution* . . . (Canberra, 1942), for a discussion of the fourteen proposed amendments. The entire proceedings of the convention are valuable for the light they shed on Australian federalism.

[12] Quoted in Melbourne *Sun*, September 30, 1961, p. 9.

[13] Colin Clark would disagree with that statement. Writing in 1956-1957, he declared that politicians in general and "teachers of history and politics

time premier of South Australia, may now well be representative of most Australians. Playford has long maintained that "centralisation would lead to inefficiency of administration, would promote bureaucracy, and would be substantially more expensive than the present system."[14] In any case, a sort of federal-state balance seems to have been reached. The Commonwealth government at Canberra remains powerful—the senior (and moneyed) partner—but the states retain a considerable degree of independence and of power. If they are junior partners, they are partners nonetheless and are so recognized in Canberra. The states have not sunk into desuetude, as some predicted they would, nor have they become mere toadies to the Commonwealth, "indigent and irresponsible satellites whose chief role is to distribute the money raised by the Federal government."[15] Australians have evidently rejected the proposition that their nation is too small in population and too poor in resources to support seven virile governments. They have decided instead that their Constitution intended "the survival and effective usefulness both of the original communities which . . . united in the federation and of the new community which their union . . . created,"[16] and thus that they will keep the states active and important governmentally.

Their decision is the product of the long tradition behind the colony-states, of the hold the states have on popular feelings, of the constitutional safeguards that surround the states, and of the vested interests of state political leaders and administrative personnel in the preservation and full use of the states. But more than anything else, their decision is the

in the Australian universities" were "to a man . . . fanatical unificationists." Colin Clark, *Australian Hopes and Fears* (London, 1958), p. 107. The author did not find this to be the case, however, in his interviews in the fall of 1961.

[14] *Convention on Alteration of Constitution*, p. 69.
[15] John D. Pringle, *Australian Accent* (London, 1958), p. 51.
[16] Hancock, *Australia*, p. 119.

product of the actual position of power that the states occupy
in the Australian Commonwealth today.

Importance of the States

The states, first of all, are the units on which the national
party system is based.[17] Despite the enlargement of the federal
role on the governmental stage, politics have remained "in
many ways, obstinately regional. This has been particularly
noticeable in the field of political leadership." Thus the
outstanding political figures in Australian history, Professor
Miller points out, have remained in the states, only occasionally moving into federal leadership, as such.[18] Moreover, the
states, taken together, are the largest employers of labor in
the Commonwealth, accounting for roughly one-sixth of all
civilian employment in Australia.[19] More important still, a
number of areas of state power under the Constitution are
central to Australian advance in the years ahead. Internal
development is perhaps Australia's most pressing need, and it
is chiefly the responsibility of the states. Agriculture and food
production in particular are the province of the states, as is
soil conservation. Education, especially higher education, is
another great need, and it too lies chiefly with the states.
The list could be easily expanded.[20] And even if initiative
and financial support in quite a number of key policy areas
have largely shifted to Canberra, the responsibility for solving
detailed problems of administration—of converting programs

[17] S. R. Davis (ed.), *The Government of the Australian States* (Sydney,
1960), p. ix.

[18] J. D. B. Miller, *Australian Government and Politics* (London, 1954),
p. 50.

[19] Australian News and Information Bureau, *Australia in Facts and Figures,*
No. 76 (December quarter 1962), p. 31. There were 396,700 men and
106,000 women working for state governments in December 1962 out of a
total employed work force of 3,167,000 persons.

[20] See the list of state functions prepared by R. S. Parker in "The Government of New South Wales," and the list prepared by A. F. Davies in
"The Government of Victoria," their chapters in Davis (ed.), *Government
of Australian States,* pp. 153–55, 177–81, respectively.

on paper into programs in fact—still rests in large part with the states. The Commonwealth's function is more to plan and finance than to operate. In addition, the Australian people have come to look to the states to look after the particular interests of their citizens. According to Professor Miller, they have to all intents and purposes charged the states with seeing that their regions hold their own in the race for development and expansion.[21] Finally, the states are important because local government is notoriously weak in Australia and its share of the governmental job is a minor one; the states therefore handle most of the functions that in the United States are assigned to local governments.

In none of these areas is it likely that the states will diminish in importance in the years to come. As state services and state activities increase, as they probably will in the course of the overall enlargement of the role of government that is taking place everywhere in the world, the states should hold their own, if not actually increase considerably in significance.

The federal "balance" that prevails in Australia today probably cannot be defended as either perfect or permanent. Australians recognize the changing nature of federalism, even as Americans do, and they are not disturbed by it. And they have learned that it is not necessary to count each Commonwealth "gain" or state "loss" on some master scoreboard but instead that what is important is that the federal system as a whole retain its vitality. The prospect that it will do so is very good. Indeed, it would appear that "for many a year to come, [federalism] will have to be taken account of, shaping and being shaped by personalities, as a democratic people continues to doubt and question, to seek after certainty, for the benefit of Australia."[22]

Because questions about its role have been so much before them through the years, federalism has remained a topic of consuming interest to Australians. Students of government,

---

[21] Miller, *Australian Government and Politics*, pp. 100, 142.
[22] Davies, "Changing Needs," p. 65.

politicians, the press, and the public at large have all been intrigued with the subject, and the result is a surprisingly large body of literature for so young an enterprise.[23] All aspects of federalism in Australia have not received equal attention, however. Its constitutional aspects have been well explored, for example, and so have many of its political aspects. And the relations between the Commonwealth government and the governments of the states—particularly in the financial field—have received some attention.

Lack of Interstate Studies

Interstate relations, on the other hand, have been almost completely ignored. The literature on that subject, indeed, is so sparse that neither "Interstate Relations" nor "Interstate Cooperation" appears as a normal library card catalogue entry anywhere in Australia. At the National Library of Australia in Canberra, the card catalogue does contain the heading "Interstate Agreement," as does that in the library of the Australian National University. But in spite of the fact that there are by now several formal interstate agreements, and a large number of informal agreements, among Australian states, the single entry under "Interstate Agreement" in both catalogues is my book on the administration of interstate compacts in the United States! "Interstate Conference" is a heading in two or three catalogues, but reports of only a few early interstate conferences are listed. Nor do indexes to periodicals,

[23] For a general discussion of the literature on federalism, see S. R. Davis and Colin A. Hughes, "The Literature of Australian Government and Politics," *Australian Journal of Politics and History*, IV (August 1958), 111–15. Representative selections from the literature include *Report of the Royal Commission on the Constitution* (1929); Greenwood, *Future of Australian Federalism*; Hancock, *Australia*, especially Chapter VI; Geoffrey Sawer and others, *Federalism in Australia* (Melbourne, 1949); F. A. Bland, "Federalism in Australia," *Public Administration*, VI (September 1946), 152–61; E. J. B. Foxcroft, "The Changing Balance of Government in Australia," *ibid.*, VI (December 1946), 184–92; and J. D. B. Miller, "More Federalism," *ibid.*, VII (March 1947), 265–72.

or to state and federal statutes, to Australian law reviews, or even to textbooks in Australian government, carry "interstate" headings. It is not merely that the present status of interstate relations is thus neglected; little or no work has ever been done in the field. No one has looked at the history of the constitutional conventions, for example, to see what the framers' expectations concerning interstate relations might have been, and no one has explored the subject in the formative years of the federation. Even in research currently being done in Australia, interstate relations tend to be neglected. Thus, in a recent series of articles[24] on seven departments of the government of New South Wales, all of which are involved in a number of relations with sister departments in other states, no mention at all is made of interstate relations.

The subject has very likely been neglected—in part, at least —because the whole field of state government has been neglected in Australia. For years, Australian scholars evinced no interest in the subject at all. Only in 1960 was anything like an adequate treatment of the subject published,[25] and for several of the states the material it contains is virtually all that is available even now. But the failure to study interstate relations has not been solely because of lack of interest. Even in Davis' study, no mention at all is made of the many interstate activities that are currently being carried on in Australia. The contributors to that volume must have assumed, like others before them, that intergovernmental relations were vertical only—between the central government and the states —and were not very important at that. Perhaps the possibility of the existence of significant horizontal relations between the states themselves was overlooked, and because they were not seen, such relations were assumed not to exist. Or interstate relations may have been ignored because as they developed, they tended to remain informal and often ad hoc, more a

[24] *Public Administration*, XX (March 1961), 33–96.
[25] Davis (ed.), *Government of the Australian States*.

matter of administrative procedure than of law, more an exercise in practical politics than in political theory, and thus were not very obvious. Or perhaps their neglect in Australia was merely a part of the general neglect of the subject in all federal systems, for although states have worked together for a good many years in both the United States and Canada, recognition of their relations as a subject for study has only recently come about.[26]

Need for Study

Whatever the reason, it is time that interstate relations were recognized in Australia. The future of the states and of their role in Australian life now seems assured, and if, as appears likely, interstate cooperation is to become as useful a tool in the solution of problems of state government "down under" as it already has in Canada and the United States, it is necessary that the present status and future possibilities of interstate relations be explored and understood. Interstate relations are too important an aspect of government to be ignored any longer. They need to be brought out of the chimney corner of Australian government and administration and carefully examined and appraised in order for their fullest potential to be realized. This volume is an attempt to fill that need.

The Setting of Interstate Relations

If in some ways interstate relations in Australia seem to have a great deal in common with interstate and inter-provincial relations in the United States and Canada, the context in which they have so far developed and will develop

---

[26] See the author's "Interprovincial Co-operation: Neglected Aspect of Canadian Federalism," *Canadian Public Administration*, II (June 1959), 83-99; the author and Redding S. Sugg, Jr., *The Administration of Interstate Compacts* (Baton Rouge, 1959).

in the future is quite different. For one thing, there are only six Australian states as compared with fifty states in the United States and ten provinces in Canada. And those six are so divided geographically that there is little meaningful physical contact between most of them. Tasmania, of course, is an island; equally isolated is the inhabited portion of Western Australia, separated from the rest of the nation by almost two thousand miles of desert or by the formidable Great Australian Bight. Nowhere does South Australia touch its neighbors where contact counts save at the southern part of her boundary with New South Wales and Victoria. And New South Wales and Queensland meet each other largely at remote and barren points in the outback. All this virtually rules out the joint undertaking of public works by two or more states, long common interstate activities in the United States. Furthermore, a large part of the Australian continent—something like one-fifth of the whole—is occupied by a federal territory, which has little likelihood of being advanced to statehood for many years, if ever. Driven wedgelike down into the center of the continent, it constitutes an effective barrier to the development of interstate contacts. At the same time, its presence and the presence of the Australian Capital Territory (Canberra) in the state of New South Wales demand the participation of the Commonwealth government in whatever interstate relations might be developed between the states which border on them.

Differences between the States

Moreover, the Australian states—again perhaps because there are so few of them—are more pronounced in their inequality than are their American counterparts.[27] Two of

27 See the remarks on the inequality of the local units in federal systems in general, in Alexander Brady, "Federations: The Canadian and British West Indian," in A. R. M. Lower and others, Evolving Canadian Federalism (Durham, 1958), p. 177; see also Hancock, Australia, p. 103.

them, indeed, are in a class by themselves. Thus the 1961 census, like all those before it, showed that well over half the total population of Australia (6,847,151 out of 10,508,191) lived in the two southeastern states of New South Wales and Victoria.[28] In addition, nature conspired to endow the two southeastern states more richly than their sisters. Not only does more rain fall there and more water flow—although parts of both states beyond the Great Dividing Range share the parched condition common to so much of Australia—but their natural resources are in better supply. The Newcastle coal basin supplies about four-fifths of the nation's coal. Gold was plentiful in Victoria and has been found in nearly all parts of New South Wales. The lead and zinc fields near Broken Hill in New South Wales are among the largest and richest in the world. Limestone, silver, copper, and iron are also mined in both states. Although the other states are not without resources (oil has recently been found in Queensland), the most favorable combination of resources at least for industrialization happens to occur in New South Wales and Victoria. Nor is that all. New South Wales and Victoria have history on their side as well. Australia's colonial experience was entirely different from that of the North American colonies. New South Wales, settled in 1788, was the original and only colony in Australia for many years. The act creating New South Wales provided, however, for the creation of other colonies, and under its terms Tasmania pulled away in 1825,

[28] The comparative populations of the units of the Australian Commonwealth are as follows:

New South Wales	3,916,907
Victoria	2,930,244
Queensland	1,518,859
South Australia	969,258
Western Australia	736,624
Tasmania	350,332
Northern Territory	27,139
Canberra (A. C. T.)	58,828

Australia in Facts and Figures, No. 71 (September quarter 1961), p. 54.

Victoria in 1851, and Queensland in 1859.[29] Only South Australia and Western Australia were born outside the family, so to speak, Western Australia having been settled independently in 1829 and South Australia in 1834. As a consequence, New South Wales has considered herself to be the senior state since the beginning, and as befits her status as the parent of three children, she claims the premier position in the Commonwealth. Her representatives at conferences called by the Commonwealth government always take the seat of honor at the right of the host and are accorded the privilege of speaking first. But Victoria made up quickly for her late start. Because of the discovery of gold there shortly after she became independent of New South Wales, and of the influx of population that followed hard upon it, Victoria attained second place in the Commonwealth overnight. Before long, her representatives at Commonwealth conferences began to occupy the seat at the host's left, and those from the other states, to their chagrin and irritation, were forced to take seats further down the table. New South Wales and Victoria seemed to them to constitute a "big league" from which they were excluded, and they felt their exclusion and their junior status very keenly. The result has been a longstanding feeling of resentment and even of hostility toward the two dominant states on the part of the others, which reveals itself in many ways in the government of the Commonwealth and which has obvious effects upon the development of harmonious interstate relations.

But the division between the "principal" states and the others is not the only division between the states in Australia. Perhaps the hardiest interstate rivalry is that between the two major states themselves. Some would go further and call it enmity. Certainly, history saw to it that there would be no

[29] See Edward Sweetman, *Australian Constitutional Development* (Melbourne, 1925), especially Chapters XVII and XXI–XXV, for a discussion of the breaking away and establishment of the five "junior" states.

love lost between the two, despite their shared preeminence. Victoria was for years stoutly protectionist; New South Wales was as vigorously free trade. Thus they worked at cross-purposes in their demands on the British Parliament before 1901 and in the Commonwealth Parliament thereafter. Nor did it please New South Wales that by 1860 Victoria had outstripped her in both population and wealth or that Victoria maintained her supremacy for almost thirty years. Finally, about 1890, New South Wales pulled ahead again, and it was Victoria's turn to feel outdone. New South Wales has stayed ahead in the race, although just recently, Victoria has picked up again. Her population increased 5.08 percent faster than that of New South Wales between the 1954 census and that of 1961, and Melbourne, long the financial and for many years the political capital of the Commonwealth, is nipping at Sydney's heels to gain the title of largest city in Australia. The result is a refueling of the flames of contest. And neither state has forgotten the bitter struggle between them over the location of the capital of the Commonwealth. As the mother state, New South Wales insisted that it be located somewhere within her boundaries. But Victorian pride "abhorred the idea of government from Sydney."[30] The two states bickered about it for almost ten years before they reached an agreement, and even after Canberra was chosen, New South Wales resented the slow transfer of governmental functions from Melbourne. The people of the two states have been brought up to have a healthy respect for the rivalry between them and do their best to keep it alive.

Nor are the differences between New South Wales and Victoria the only ones between the states. Thus Professor Morrison is at pains to point out in the very first paragraph of his chapter on the government of Queensland the characteristic belief among local citizens that the state and its

[30] Hancock, *Australia*, p. 278.

people are in many ways quite different from other Australians and to mention their conviction that matters affecting their State can be decided only by Queenslanders and that one must live in the state for some years to understand its problems.[31] One does not have to be in Queensland very long, moreover, to encounter an expression of the bitterness that still lingers toward New South Wales for her treatment of Queensland before separation. Tasmania and Western Australia are still remote from the rest of the country, and their interests and concerns consequently are still somewhat alien to those of their more cosmopolitan sister states. Tasmania is perhaps the most self-conscious of all the states. Nowhere in the Commonwealth, Professor Townsley remarks, is the state flag displayed more often or the state name used so frequently in some form or other as a Christian name; nowhere else is there quite so strongly developed "a sense of regional difference."[32] Western Australia entered the federation only grudgingly and voted once to secede from it.[33] For many years the high protective tariff levied on goods brought into the eastern states caused Western Australia to complain "that it was being taxed for the good of eastern industrialists."[34] Though time and more frequent contact with the east have softened her feelings somewhat, there is still widespread in Western Australia a conviction that as the federation has developed, the older and more populous states have been able to exploit the smaller states, particularly Western

[31] A. A. Morrison, "The Government of Queensland," in Davis (ed.), *Government of Australian States*, p. 249; see also Sir Raphael Cilento and Clem Lack (eds.), *Triumph in the Tropics* (Brisbane, 1959), *passim*. However, in "Queensland—One Hundred Years," *Current Affairs Bulletin*, XXIV (August 3, 1959), 98, these assertions are questioned, and "a very thorough examination of the State's history . . . to determine whether they have any validity" is called for.

[32] W. A. Townsley, "The Government of Tasmania," in Davis (ed.), *Government of Australian States*, pp. 554–55.

[33] See E. D. Watt, "Secession in Western Australia," *University Studies in Western Australian History* (Perth, 1958), pp. 43–86.

[34] R. M. Crawford, *Australia* (London, 1952), p. 172.

Australia.[35] As for South Australia, she began in nonconformity and was the only one of the colonies never to import convicts.[36] Because of this, South Australia has been accused by other Australians of having a slight sense of superiority.[37] Moreover, South Australia developed along different lines than most of the other states. Her population became balanced "as to occupation and wealth" sooner than that of any other colony, with the result that the "pastoralists never gained the . . . predominance in wealth and power which they enjoyed in the eastern colonies."[38] This difference cast South Australian politics into an independent mold before federation, and she has continued to practice a high degree of political independence ever since.

The differences between the states are not new. They go back to colonial times. Thus Geoffrey Rawson describes the early Australian colonies in the following terms: "each separate community pursued its busy, quiet, remote path alone . . . intent on [its] own domestic problems, on cultivating [its] own garden. . . . [The colonies] were . . . jealous of their own domains and of each other, each building up its own panoply of state authority. These small and isolated communities developed an intense political fervour. . . . [The] interests and the preoccupations of one . . . were different from and in many ways opposed to those of another. There was rivalry approaching enmity; parochialism was rampant. . . . The spirit of unity was absent. . . . Australia consisted of 'six disunited and discordant colonies.' "[39]

Nor did anything force the disputing colonies together. No single issue, such as the slavery issue in the United States, arose to draw colonies together into a common cause, nor

[35] J. C. Willcock, Premier of Western Australia, in *Convention on Alteration of Constitution*, p. 74.
[36] See Douglas Pike, *Paradise of Dissent, South Australia, 1829-1857* (Melbourne, 1957).
[37] Clark, *Australian Hopes and Fears*, pp. 20, 33.
[38] Crawford, *Australia*, p. 81.
[39] Geoffrey Rawson, *Australia* (London, 1948), pp. 75-76.

was any provision made when the later colonies were established for any form of cooperation between them. Instead, the colonies continued on their separate ways, "completely independent of each other, free to raise hostile tariff walls and to build railways with different gauges . . . [and] to go their own way in tackling the urgent problems that beset them."[40] Even when they finally joined in federation, they remained "jealously watchful of their own individual rights, responsibilities and privileges."[41]

Not even the party system helped pull the states much nearer to one another. Certainly part of the reason for the long hostility between New South Wales and Victoria has been the fact that Victoria has been fairly consistently Liberal, whereas New South Wales has been more often than not Labour. To this day, Australian politics are characterized by a variety of local and regional variations. South Australia plays its own game of politics and has no close ties with parties outside the state. Queensland is in the odd position of having a unique split in her Labour party and has been governed by a Liberal-Country coalition since 1957.[42] Tasmania is the only state that has kept a rather fine balance between the two major parties through the years, but there is a distinctive Tasmanian twist to Labour and Liberal policies even there. Perhaps the only case where party politics has been a unifying tie is between New South Wales and Western Australia. Both have been Labour over the years, and a New South Wales Labour premier even served as a sort of mentor and guide to at least one Western Australian Labour premier. But geography has made the compatibility between those two states relatively meaningless.

Nor does commerce serve as a link to bind the states in Australia to one another the way it does in the United States.

[40] A. G. L. Shaw, *The Story of Australia* (London, 1960), p. 130.
[41] Rawson, *Australia*, p. 78.
[42] See Clem Lack (ed.), *Three Decades of Queensland Political History, 1929–1960* (Brisbane, 1962), Parts VIII and IX.

Professor Hancock noted the presence of large "areas of . . . marked economic individuality" when he wrote his landmark book about Australia in 1930, and went on to report that "In contrast with the United States of America, Australia has an inconsiderable amount of interstate trade; a glance at a railway map will show how the channels of trade run within the various State boundaries, up and down from the interior to the sea."[43] The situation had not changed much when Colin Clark wrote in 1957 that "in the present state of Australian transport, the Australian manufacturer finds that the population and industries of a neighbouring Australian State might almost as well be in Europe, for all the good they can do him as markets or suppliers. . . . This is literally true. The freight rates on sending goods between one Australian State and another are as high, in some cases higher, than the cost of sending goods to or from Europe or North America, and, in addition to the cost, the uncertainties and delays of shipping have a considerable effect upon the manufacturer."[44] Until well into the future, lines of commercial intercourse will probably continue to flow outward rather than inward, knitting Australia ever closer to Europe and the United States in the process but leaving the six Australian states still rather independent economic units.

Although it is tempting to carry still further a description of the forces dividing the Australian states—and the literature will still yield a number of other examples[45]—it is not necessary to do so to make the point that there are a good many divisive influences at work among the Australian states and that they have operated for quite a long time, with the result

[43] Hancock, *Australia*, p. 124.
[44] Clark, *Australian Hopes and Fears*, p. 72.
[45] See James Bryce, *Studies in History and Jurisprudence* (New York, 1901), pp. 404–405; Ernestine Hill, *Water into Gold* (Melbourne, 1937), *passim*; Sir Harold Clapp, "Australia—A Nation," *Public Administration*, VI (September 1946), 147–51.

that an atmosphere of conscious state differentiation must be taken into account in any study involving Australian state government. Certainly the existence of so many differences and the glee with which the citizens of the several states seem determined to maintain them go far to explain why interstate relations were long in developing and why they have been neglected in Australian research and writing on government and administration. Important though these differences are, however, they should not be made too much of. The colonies did after all come together into a federation, and the states have stayed together ever since. In the process, a great deal of national pride has developed, and an Australian consciousness is very much in evidence throughout the country. Despite the obstacles interstate differences have presented and still offer, interstate relations and cooperation have grown steadily until they have come to occupy an important place in the Australian pattern of government, so important a place that an understanding of their role is necessary for a full understanding of Australian federalism as it operates today.

Chapter 2 THE CONTEXT OF
INTERSTATE RELATIONS:
A PATTERN OF COOPERATION

Because there are no historical studies of interstate relations
to draw upon, it is not easy to trace their development in
Australia. It is probable, however, that they developed rather
slowly. For not only did federation fail to remove automatically the many differences between the colonies, in some
cases it only exacerbated them. Western Australia and her
dissatisfaction with her financial position in the Commonwealth is an excellent case in point. The development of ties
between any of the states, for that matter, had to wait until
communications and transportation improved enough so that
interstate contact was possible on more than a sporadic basis.
And this did not come about until the extensive use of air
travel. Although World War I did for a little while bring
Australia to a new peak of national sentiment,[1] it did not
give the states so strong a sense of a common threat as did
the Great Depression and World War II. So serious was the
threat of the latter that Australia acted as one nation as never
before in her history, and in the process many Australians in
public life—particularly in the state services—for the first time
began to lose some of their chauvinism and to feel conscious
of the possibilities of interstate planning and action. In any
case, interstate relations as they exist today in Australia seem
to be primarily the product of relatively recent times.

It would have been odd indeed if there had not been some
development of interstate relations even from the outset, for
despite their willful independence, the colonies had had some
experience in cooperation. As early as 1847, Earl Grey sug-

gested some machinery for cooperation between the colonies.
"Grey feared the consequences of intercolonial tariffs with
customs houses on the border," and as a way of preventing
them from being built, he proposed the creation of a body of
representatives from all the colonies to supervise a commercial
union, intercolonial communications, and such other common interests as from time to time might arise.[2] But Grey
was before his time. The "reluctant particularistic colonies,"
Professor Hancock commented, thought the proposal hardly
worth considering.[3] And Grey's idea received no warmer a
response in England. In deference to general criticism, he
abandoned the scheme.[4] In 1849 the Privy Council Committee for Trade and Foreign Plantations, which was then
drafting an Australian Colonies Government Bill, wrote in a
provision for a general assembly of the colonies, the members
of which would be appointed by the several colonial legislatures to deal with matters of common interest to all. But the
provision was withdrawn in the House of Lords after heavy
criticism in both houses.[5] The idea of the colonies overcoming
their differences enough to work together for certain common
purposes continued to appeal to many, however, and if Lord
Bryce was right, "it received a certain impulse from the
creation of the Canadian Confederation in 1867."[6]

The Federal Council of 1885

By 1883, it appeared that the time was finally ripe for
action. A conference of delegates from all Britain's Aus-

1 Crawford, *Australia*, p. 166.
2 Shaw, *Story of Australia*, p. 129.
3 Hancock, *Australia*, p. 65.
4 See John M. Ward, *Earl Grey and the Australian Colonies, 1846–1857*
(Melbourne, 1958).
5 See Sir Robert Garran, "The Federation Movement and the Founding
of the Commonwealth," Chapter XV in *The Cambridge History of the
British Empire* (Cambridge, 1933), Vol. VII, Pt. 1; see also Brian Fitzpatrick, *The Australian Commonwealth* (Melbourne, 1956), p. 90.
6 Bryce, *Studies*, p. 395.

tralasian colonies was held in Sydney that year, and its recommendations were sent on to England. After extensive consultation with colonial leaders,[7] Parliament embodied the bulk of the recommendations in the Federal Council of Australasia Act, 1885.[8] The act combined all the Australasian colonies —Fiji and New Zealand as well as the Australian colonies—into a loose unit, under a council empowered to deal with certain matters of common concern to them all. The act made it clear that no interference with any colony's management of its own internal affairs was to be tolerated. It called for the council to meet biennially; with the agreement of the governors of three colonies, special sessions might be held. The council was to consist of two members per colony, who were to be appointed by the legislature of the colony, according to its terms. The council's legislative authority extended specifically to the relations of Australia with the Pacific Islands,[9] preventing an influx of criminals into the colonies, regulating fisheries beyond territorial limits, serving legal process in the several colonies, enforcing judgments throughout the area, and taking criminal offenders into custody. In addition, any colonial legislature could request Her Majesty in council to submit items to the council, and if any two colonial legislatures agreed, the subjects of general defense, quarantine, patents, copyrights, bills of exchange and promissory notes, uniform weights and measures, marriage and divorce, naturalization, regulation of joint stock companies, and intercolonial relations generally might be referred to the council. Any legislation passed by the council had to be referred to the governors of each of the colonies for assent, and it was subject to a further veto in London. The council acts that were

[7] See British Sessional Papers, House of Commons, 1884-1885, LIV, passim.
[8] 48 and 49 Victoria, Chapter 60 (1885).
[9] The occasion of the Sydney Conference was the movements France was making that seemed to indicate an interest in acquiring New Hebrides. There was also concern that Germany was becoming interested in Papua. Bryce, Studies, p. 395.

approved, however, were to become law in each colony and were to supersede any contrary laws that might happen to be on the books. The colonies could also use the council to make representations to Her Majesty's government whenever they chose to do so. In order to be effective in any colony, the act creating the council had to be accepted by that colony's legislature. Original involvement was thus voluntary. Four colonies were enthusiastic supporters of the act from the beginning—Victoria, Queensland, Tasmania, and Western Australia[10]—and they immediately adopted it and set the council in motion. It met nine times in the next dozen years, but to little avail, for New South Wales was not in favor of the idea at all and never did accept it. Neither did Fiji or New Zealand. The council, thus only partially representative even of the Australian colonies, had little chance of success. As the agent general for New Zealand in London wrote the undersecretary of state for colonies, "A federation of Australia, with New South Wales left out, will never work."[11] Without the support and participation of the mother state, and with no effective executive of its own and no power to collect revenue, it was doomed from the start.[12]

From the point of view of interstate relations, however, the council was not a total failure, for representatives of four of the colonies continued to hold fairly regular consultations with each other, thus reinforcing the trend toward intercolonial conferences that was then developing.

One of the first intercolonial conferences had been held in 1863 to discuss the improvement of the Murray River for navigation. Thereafter, state officials began to meet for a variety of purposes. In the course of their discussions, they covered a great many points—an intercolonial customs union, defense and Pacific affairs, restriction of alien entry into

---

[10] Fitzpatrick, *Australian Commonwealth*, p. 90.

[11] *British Sessional Papers, House of Commons*, 1884–1885, LIV, 32.

[12] See Bryce, *Studies*, p. 396; see also Garran, "The Federation Movement," pp. 427–29.

Australia, and the need for uniform action in a number of social, industrial, and transportation areas. By 1890, federation itself had become something to talk about on these occasions. Although very little concrete in the way of results was to be seen from these conferences, colonial leaders did have the experience of working together and of listening to and sometimes being persuaded by another point of view. Indeed, the creation of the Commonwealth and the Commonwealth Constitution were very likely the direct results of many interstate conventions of state parliamentary leaders in the fifteen to twenty years preceding 1901.[13] There would be from these meetings a certain amount of carryover which could be applied to interstate relations. The habit of intercolonial action was not confined to state officials. The first Intercolonial Trades Union Congress was held in 1879, and by the time of the second congress in 1884, it was taken for granted that cooperative action between state unions would be forthcoming.[14] Not to be outdone, employers also formed intercolonial associations.[15] The frequency of consultation across state lines was as outstanding as its variety by the time of federation. The example was not lost in the years ahead.

The Commonwealth Evolves

By 1901, the Australian people were becoming more conscious of what they had in common than of their differences. As they progressed through the nineteenth century, they had managed to escape the regional differences that in the United States had led to civil war and to the perpetuation of grievances long after the last shot had been fired, and in

[13] This idea was expressed most succinctly to me by A. Lyell McEwin, Chief Secretary, Minister of Health and Minister of Mines, South Australia, in his letter to me of January 8, 1960.
[14] Hancock, Australia, p. 200; R. Gollan, Radical and Working Class Politics: A Study of Eastern Australia 1850–1910 (Melbourne, 1960), pp. 94–96.
[15] Crawford, Australia, p. 139.

Canada to a permanent rift between two parts of the community. Geography helped the Australians a great deal. Except for Tasmania and the corner of Queensland, Australian terrain is remarkably uniform. Even the flora and fauna remain the same. An Australian found himself at home in terms of environment almost anywhere on the continent. As development continued, the settlers added few manmade distinctions to set one region off from another. Houses and public buildings, the layout of towns, and the construction of sheep stations followed a common pattern everywhere in Australia. In such surroundings, it was only natural for a community of interest and feeling to develop and to grow steadily through the years, until no observer of the Australian scene could fail to note the existence of "a community . . . viewpoint" as "one of the basic facts about Australia."[16]

The growth of that community was obviously abetted by the common nationality of the Australian colonists. Lord Bryce commented that at the time of the federation, Australia was "almost as purely English as Massachusetts, Connecticut, and Virginia were in 1776, and probably more English than were the thirteen original States taken as a whole."[17] And until well after World War II, a predominant percentage of the immigrants to Australia continued to be British. Bound together by a single language and a common social background—the very fact that many of the first Australians had been convicts provided a point of unity from the beginning—the Australians were never really set apart from one another. Moreover, they brought with them a common pattern of law and government, and if they created six independent colonies, each colony was nevertheless very much like every other in the way it went about its political and administrative business and in the application of the rule of law. These factors alone, Attorney General Sir Garfield

16 Fred Alexander, "Australia," in Kenneth Bradley (ed.), *The Living Commonwealth* (London, 1961), p. 164.
17 Bryce, *Studies*, pp. 405–406.

Barwick commented in 1961, were sufficient to give an early "sound basis for the success of . . . federalism in Australia."[18]

It was not long until Australia, the land, infected the blood of the British settlers, and as the years went by, although they might still refer to England as home, they more and more came to think of themselves as Australians, as being a new breed of man. Australian literature and poetry began to reflect this growing nationalism even before federation,[19] and World War I made Australia fully conscious of itself and of its own identity and proud of the nation that had been created under the Southern Cross.[20] Australians everywhere understood that it was an Australian legend they had developed, "not a Victorian or West Australian or Queensland legend; for [they] were at root alike in the manner of life [they] lived . . . and in their general attachment to the assumptions of a democratic egalitarian society."[21] Mateship came to have a meaning in Australia that it acquired nowhere else, and Australians from one end of the continent to the other felt its pull.

All of these forces combined to support Australia's political leaders as they made their first steps into federation and to strengthen the new union. As the years went by, they continued to operate to break down barriers between the states and eventually to make interstate cooperation a reality.

Interstate Cooperation

There were other forces at work for harmonious interstate relations as well. If Queensland remained remote from

[18] Quoted in the New York *Times*, February 19, 1961, p. 50.
[19] See Crawford, *Australia*, Chapter IX, for a general discussion of "The Australian Legend."
[20] See A. B. ("Banjo") Patterson, *The Man from Snowy River and Other Verses* (Sydney, 1961), for a classic example of Australian self-expression.
[21] Crawford, *Australia*, p. 148.

Tasmania and Western Australia, and they from her—even the airplane has not tied them together to the degree that it has the other states—a number of alignments grew up between the other colony-states that served to counterbalance the pressures that held them apart. New South Wales and Victoria, however much they were rivals, nevertheless came to be linked in what amounted to an industrial and commercial partnership that dominated Australia's economic scene. Their viewpoints on a surprising number of important issues were thus virtually identical because the same economic interests were involved. Similarly, a strong attachment between Western Australia and Tasmania developed early. As the two poorest colonies and the two regular claimant states in the Commonwealth, they formed a community of interest that defied the barriers of sea and sand. Tasmania and Victoria likewise had a close relationship. The original settlement of Victoria was overseas from Tasmania rather than overland from New South Wales, and the two states have maintained a special regard for each other ever since, the most obvious evidence of which today is perhaps the state lottery that Victoria conducts for Tasmania. Queensland and New South Wales are similarly tied together. However much bad feeling remains as a result of Queensland's colonial experience as the dumping ground for second offenders from New South Wales, the fact remains that Queensland is chiefly a primary producer and is dependent on New South Wales for the bulk of the manufactured goods she uses. Even in the primary field, Queensland and New South Wales have special ties. Queensland is the leading producer of sugar in Australia, and by special arrangement with New South Wales, all sugar processed there is acquired by Queensland, which assures her of an almost complete sugar monopoly. And at least some kind of a case can be made for a connection between Queensland and South Australia, if only because the cattlemen in Western Queensland look to Adelaide rather than to Brisbane for their markets, since Birdsville, the center of the cattle country, is nearer to the South Australian capital than it is to Brisbane.

If none of these attractions had existed to draw the Australian states together, they would probably have developed a community of feeling anyway as a result of their common position vis-à-vis the Commonwealth government. There is a common saying in Australia that the only time the states unite is when they go to Canberra, and the saying has a certain amount of truth in it. Time and time again the states have first found common ground between them on a particular issue when they have joined in insistence on or in opposition to some proposed Commonwealth policy. Almost every state political figure in Australia is frank to admit that interstate differences give way in the face of the necessity for a united state approach to the Commonwealth, which holds a stronger bargaining position than any of the states alone. Oddly enough, the states are more apt to come together in a stand *for* a Commonwealth program than *against* an exertion of Commonwealth power. In this respect, the Australian situation is the reverse of the American, for one thing the states in America will unite on is to defend "states' rights" against "federal encroachment." The Australian states have never been unduly bothered by the exercise of Commonwealth power, and indeed are apt to demand that the Commonwealth do more than it has been doing rather than less. On the other hand, when questions arise concerning interpretation of the Australian Constitution, which affect the rights of the states and the Commonwealth *inter se*, the states almost always join hands to protect their interests. In either case, the facts that their interests in relation to the Commonwealth are more often than not the same and that in union there is strength serve to persuade the states to overlook a good deal of interstate difference and to act in cooperation.

Common sense alone would seem to dictate a certain amount of interstate collaboration and cooperation. The states are not after all sworn enemies; they are sworn instead to the creation of "one indissoluble Federal Commonwealth." Thus in the natural course of events, it is harmony, not discord, which might be expected. Certainly the areas of power left to the states under the Constitution immediately suggest cooperation. A certain amount of common action in the regulation of primary production and of industry and commerce, for example, would seem to be inevitable in a nation whose economy is steadily becoming more unified. So would cooperation in the establishment of a number of matériel standards and professional qualifications. Natural resources ignore state lines and so to some extent must programs for the conservation and development of these resources. Education, public health and welfare, and the promotion of industry all suggest other possibilities for joint action. It is too much to believe that state officials, sincerely devoted to their responsibilities, would through the years have altogether ignored the attractions of common action in any of these fields. Rather, they might have been expected— as they did in practice—to have explored them whenever the opportunity to do so presented itself.

Commonwealth-State Cooperation

This natural tendency toward interstate cooperation was strengthened by the experience of the states over a long period of time with cooperation with the Commonwealth government. Although constitutionally speaking, Commonwealth-state relations were neglected by the founding fathers—left in the "backyard of federalism," as Professor Davies puts it, with "no rules, or even suggestions about how ministers or officials should consult together when they needed complementary or common policies"[22]—the necessity of cooperation between those two levels of government very quickly became obvious, and since 1901 a wide variety of cooperative arrangements have been developed, particularly in the field of finance. Today, to a much greater degree than is generally understood, the task of Australian government is carried on by the Commonwealth and the states cooperatively.

Examples of cooperative Commonwealth-state arrangements abound. One of the most successful has been the Joint Coal Board, created in 1947 by the Commonwealth and the state of New South Wales. Perhaps the best known is the River Murray Commission, which will be discussed in another chapter. In the field of health there is a virtual labyrinth of cooperative activities.[23] With finance provided by the Commonwealth, the states have waged a campaign against tuberculosis for fifteen years. Under other arrangements, the Commonwealth assists the states in providing immunization against poliomyelitis, in providing home nursing service, and in making capital expenditures on mental institutions. At the several ports of entry to Australia, state department of agriculture officers supervise plant quarantining activities for the Commonwealth.[24] Plant quarantine publicity is handled jointly by state and Commonwealth authorities. The Commonwealth allocates a certain amount yearly (£72,500 in

[22] A. F. Davies, *Australian Democracy* (Melbourne, 1958), p. 96. Davies distinguishes four major types of Commonwealth-state cooperation (*ibid.*, pp. 97–98). See also on this general subject W. J. Campbell, *Australian State Public Finance* (Sydney, 1954), especially Chapters VIII–X, XII, XVII, and XIX; Foxcroft, "Changing Balance of Government"; F. R. E. Mauldon, "Commonwealth-State Relations in Administration," *Public Administration*, VIII (December 1949), 138-42; and Davies, "Changing Needs," pp. 48-65.

[23] See Commonwealth of Australia, *Report of the Director-General of Health, 1st July 1960—30th June 1961* (Canberra, 1951), *passim*.

[24] In his interim report in 1962 the Director General of Health for the Commonwealth went out of his way to comment on the "amicable and cooperative relationships . . . between [the state] Departments and the Commonwealth Department of Health." Commonwealth of Australia, *Interim Report by the Director-General of Health, 1961–1962* (Canberra, 1962), p. 9.

1961) to the states to assist them in their national fitness programs. The Commonwealth has established a model child-health center in each of the capital cities—Lady Gowrie Centres, they are called—which are controlled by local committees in each state with overall supervision being exercised by a committee in Canberra. And the Commonwealth subsidizes the issuance of free milk for school children by the states.

Nearly as lengthy a catalogue could be made of Commonwealth-state activities in the field of scientific research, through the Commonwealth Scientific and Industrial Research Organisation (C.S.I.R.O.), and in the field of agricultural research. The list of Commonwealth-state relations is a long one. At some point in most of them state officers are brought together, and in the course of working out vertical relations between the Commonwealth and the states, the logic of extending their work horizontally has often been persuasive. Using the pattern already set by Commonwealth-state programs—for many of the techniques and devices employed are the same—state officials have found an interstate program easy to achieve. Interstate relations, indeed, have been a natural accompaniment of Commonwealth-state relations.

Interstate Relations and the Constitution

Interstate cooperation was thus in a sense foreordained in Australia. A number of causes operated to promote it from the first days of federation, the obstacles of state differences notwithstanding, and some even predated federation. Since this is the case, it is odd that the Constitution of Australia did not provide for it. Perhaps the obvious needed no statement, in Australia, in the United States, or in Canada. In any case, the Australian Constitution is as barren of guidance in the matter as is either of the other constitutions. Just as it neglects to provide in specific terms for Commonwealth-state cooperation,[25] so it fails to enjoin interstate cooperation on the states. Although it was modeled after the Constitution of the United States, as Professor Greenwood assures us,[26] it did not even pick up the provision for interstate compacts in the American Constitution, negative though it is.[27] References to interstate matters are confined to the provision referring interstate disputes to the High Court (Section 75, iv) and to the provisions covering the rights of residents of one state while in another (Section 117) and requiring the recognition of the laws and records of one state by the others (Section 118). Beyond these familiar clauses, the Constitution has nothing to say as far as interstate relations are concerned. Nor do any of the state constitutions do any better. No Australian state constitution even implies the existence of the possibility of interstate cooperation, much less makes specific provision (like the constitutions of an increasing number of American states) for some kind of interstate governmental machinery. The Australian founding fathers, both Commonwealth and state, did not recognize the need for intergovernmental cooperation in the federal system they created, and their successors in office, so to speak, seem to have overlooked the substantial developments in that direction that have been made since federation.

Growth of Interstate Relations

If they were ignored constitutionally, however, interstate relations nevertheless went right on growing. For the most

[25] It is possible to construe Section 51, subsection xxxiv, which concerns the construction of railways, and Section 120, concerned with prisons, so that they imply Commonwealth-state cooperation.

[26] Greenwood, *Future of Australian Federalism*, pp. 32–33.

[27] The interstate compact clause of Article I, Section 10, of the Constitution of the United States says that "No State shall, without the consent of Congress . . . enter into any agreement or compact with another state."

part, they were at first and have remained voluntary and informal in nature, though in recent years a few have been given a statutory or contractual basis. Many arose simply from necessity in the day-to-day conduct of common business by state agencies. A case in point is the cooperation that early developed between state police departments. It was quickly discovered that no department could do its own job well, without the active support and cooperation of the other departments in the Commonwealth. Today an interstate network of radio communication links every department, and each department uses it regularly both to obtain assistance from a neighboring state in an emergency and to report crimes and escapes. Members of the police forces of one state serving at border stations are automatically sworn as special constables in the adjoining state or states and given the power of arrest there. Often the police of one state will carry out investigations and serve summonses and warrants for another state. So obvious is the necessity for interstate cooperation in police work that it is recognized "at all levels in the [Police] Forces, from the higher command to junior members. It is now taken for granted that if Police in one State require assistance from Police in another, that assistance is readily forthcoming, just as readily as if the request had come from any member of the same force. . . . [T]oday interstate co-operation between Police Forces could not be more complete if there were, in fact, one single Police Force in the Commonwealth."[28]

Some interstate relations have been the product of conferences and personal contact—manufactured, as it were, rather than natural. Most state agencies in Australia, as in the United States and Canada, deal with their own problems in their own way as problems arise from day to day, quite independently of what their counterparts in other states are

[28] Commissioner of Police, New South Wales, to the Under Secretary, Premier's Department, August 5, 1960.

doing. But ministers of departments and agency heads, like their American brethren, are gregarious, and like them, they early developed the habit of meeting to discuss their mutual problems. Out of that exchange has come the slow modification of practices in all the states toward a common pattern. An example here would be the kind of cooperation that has come to exist between state milk boards. On the face of it, there does not appear to be any call for cooperation between milk boards. Their function is the regulation and control of the supply and distribution of milk within the states, and every board's legal powers and responsibilities are of course confined within its own state boundaries. Somewhat similar boards have been established in all the states, however, and since World War II, conferences of the milk boards have been held biennially. These conferences make no binding decisions, but conference resolutions carry considerable weight with each of the participating boards. Between conferences, contact is maintained between the several boards by both correspondence and interstate visits. Thus, although each of the boards is legally independent of the others—and although their powers and organization are by no means identical—they operate from similar bases of fact and information and as a result their policies and practices are remarkably uniform. To all intents and purposes there is a common approach to milk board problems all across Australia.

Sources of Interstate Relations

Although it is hard to ascribe certain interstate relations to one source and others to another, it is convenient for purposes of discussion to divide their sources into five separate groups:[29] 1. Interstate relations growing out of Common-

[29] I am indebted to the Premier of Western Australia, the Honorable David Brand, for suggesting this method of classification. David Brand to author, January 29, 1960.

wealth inspired conferences and activities; 2. Interstate relations resulting from conferences and interim contacts of state ministers and department heads; 3. Interstate relations developed at meetings of groups advisory to government departments and agencies and at meetings of lay organizations with impact on governmental programs; 4. Interstate relations fostered by exchange of correspondence, visits, and information between state agencies and officials; and 5. Interstate relations characterized by formal intergovernmental arrangements between two or more states involving interstate activities. The first type of relations will form the subject of Chapter 3, the next three types will be dealt with in Chapter 4, and formal interstate arrangements will be discussed in Chapter 5. In addition, there is a new but rapidly expanding movement toward the adoption of uniform law among the states, which will form the topic of Chapter 6.

A Preliminary Survey

Whatever their source or type, most interstate relations in Australia are new enough so that they have not yet been catalogued. The Premier's Department in three of the states —New South Wales, Victoria, and Queensland—conducted a government-wide survey for me during 1960 to ascertain how widespread were interstate relations in each state, however, and this was the first time in any of the states that comprehensive data had been collected about them. The surveys in all three states showed that every department of state government had somehow become involved in interstate relations. Even state departments that do not seem to have a great deal of common ground between them on which to build reported a number of relationships. The state milk boards are one example; traffic commissions are another. The 1960 survey report of the Traffic Commission of Victoria listed thirteen different kinds of interstate contact, ranging from the regular exchange of technical reports and new traffic regulations and answering specific inquiries from counterpart authorities in other states to the representation of the commission on four Australia-wide bodies where traffic problems are discussed and ways to solve them explored. And the departments of local government in the three states reported that they regularly exchange information and grant reciprocity to locally awarded certificates and licenses. Interviews in the other three states confirmed the findings of the surveys in the east; virtually all state government departments in those states, regardless of the nature of their responsibilities, were similarly involved in some or many kinds of interstate relations.

All the states are not equally involved, however. Their departmental organization is not uniform for one thing. Although since 1946 there has been an association of state government insurance officers which holds conferences at eighteen-month intervals and has provided a fruitful forum for the development of interstate relations in that field, the State Insurance Office of South Australia does not function in anything like the same manner as those of the other states. Participation in the association has thus not been as meaningful to South Australia as to some of the others. Nor is the political climate as ripe for interstate relations in some states as in others. South Australia continues to go her independent way, and even though Playford is no longer Premier, she probably will not change her ways very much. Tasmania, on the other hand, perhaps in an attempt to overcome her isolation, took an early lead in promoting closer cooperation between the colonies, especially commercial cooperation,[30] as well as lending her support to the movement for the Federal Council of Australasia. And to this day Tasmanian leaders are likely to be found among those pressing

[30] W. A. Townsley, "The Parliament of Tasmania," in F. C. Green (ed.), *A Century of Responsible Government, 1856–1956* (Hobart, 1956), p. 12.

for additional interstate programs and activities. Her attorney general, for instance, has been in the forefront of the recent movement for uniform law. Victoria too has occasionally taken a position of leadership in pushing for interstate co-operation. New South Wales is much more apt to lag behind.

Political leadership—or even opposition—does not seem to be decisive in every case, however, for the department-by-department survey in the three eastern states showed a remarkable consistency of involvement in interstate relations. In many fields of state responsibility, of course, interstate cooperation is almost imperative, and the department concerned can hardly be restrained on political grounds from answering the call of necessity. The police commissioners in South Australia and New South Wales, for example, are as enthusiastic about interstate cooperation as are their fellow officers in Tasmania and Victoria. And despite political differences, forestry officers can be expected to approach their problems more often in harmony than not. The same is true of departments of tourism. As with forestry, this is chiefly a state responsibility in Australia, and each state maintains its own tourist organization. But tourists—from overseas at least—come to see Australia, and not just one state, and thus states must cooperate for their own sakes.

To expect perfect cooperation among the states is of course fatuous. Every contact between state officials can no more be expected to produce harmony and cooperation than con-tacts between people in any other work. Regular conferences or no, state government men do not always see eye to eye. Thus at the 1961 meeting of the Australian Transport Ad-visory Council, on which all the state transport boards are represented, the states split right down the middle over the question of Commonwealth aid to beef roads,[31] and many another interstate meeting adjourns with less than unanimity having been achieved. Even so, the survey revealed a sur-

[31] For a report of the 1961 meeting, see *Australian Facts and Figures*, No. 69 (March quarter 1961), p. 72.

prising amount of friendliness and inclination toward cooperation in state officials all the way up and down the departmental
line.

If there is both a disposition toward cooperation among
state officials generally and a quite respectable structure of
interstate relations in Australia today, interstate relations are
still far from constituting a single coordinated whole. For
the most part, not even the premiers' departments in any of
the states were aware of the extent of interstate cooperation
among state departments until they undertook the survey for
me or I questioned members of their staffs about their state's
involvement in interstate relations. There is no center in any
state where activities in the field are collected and collated.
Rather than a single edifice of interstate cooperation, what
has developed is a collection of cooperative activities being
carried on largely independently of each other on many
different levels, involving many different officials in all six
Australian states. Although the people concerned in each
field of activity may be aware of interstate relations in their
own field of interest, there is no general awareness of interstate
relations elsewhere in the government and none at all outside
it. Nor is there anything regular about the relations which
have developed. Some involve recurring activities, but others
find expression only in one isolated instance. Some involve
groups of government officials who meet at set intervals,
whereas others meet only periodically or as the need arises.
And the quality and strength of each set of relationships
vary a great deal too.

Interstate cooperation is still developing in Australia, however, and in the next few years there may be a considerable
change in this picture. The full possibilities of cooperation
in carrying out the responsibilities of strong and active states,
indeed, have only just been tapped, and as further experiments
are made, a new general description may well have to be
written. In the meantime, it is important that the present
status of interstate relations be described and analyzed.

3 INTERSTATE COOPERATION THROUGH COMMONWEALTH INSPIRATION

The Commonwealth government has assumed a position of leadership in the development of interstate relations in Australia. It has done so indirectly, for the most part, as a byproduct of meetings and activities initiated in connection with the exercise of its own powers, rather than directly as a matter of policy. Many powers of government in Australia—and particularly those called upon for use in postwar development—are concurrent under the Australian Constitution. Frequent consultation between the Commonwealth and the states is therefore required, and in the course of consulting on their joint interests with the Commonwealth, state representatives discover ways of improving or undertaking cooperative relations of their own. Indeed, consideration of interstate relations apart from Commonwealth-state relations poses a false dichotomy and leads to a misunderstanding of Australian federalism.

The Commonwealth's greatest contribution to interstate relations has perhaps been in providing an arena for their development at the meetings and conferences it convenes at frequent intervals. The Commonwealth government did not originate the conference device, of course. Interstate conferences have constituted an important factor in intergovernmental cooperation since prefederation days, and they continued to be held off and on in the years after 1901. But since World War II they have increased in number and significance. Prior to the war, the interest the Commonwealth and the states had in one another was limited largely to finances, and though a good many conferences were held on that subject in the depression years especially, the need for intergovernmental action—and thus for conferences—in other areas did not seem so pressing. After the war, however, the pent-up needs of the Australian people combined with the great surge of development that the war forced upon Australia to require the Commonwealth to direct its attention to the solution of a great many accumulated problems. As it sought ways to attack them through government action, the first step in many cases (and an important step in others) was a conference of the persons at both levels of government most concerned with their solution. So frequently were such conferences called that they shortly became a habit, and they have continued to be used ever since. A number of them have been absorbed into the formal process of government and are recognized as official, at least to the extent of being listed as Commonwealth functions in the Commonwealth *Directory*.

Premiers' Conferences

The best known of the official conferences was already a well established going concern long before World War II. The Premiers' Conference, as a matter of fact, is rooted in the custom of occasionally conferring on matters of mutual interest that was established by colonial premiers well before federation. After federation, the conferences were continued and expanded, particularly under the chairmanship of Premier William A. Holman[1] of New South Wales, and they early came to be regarded as major political events. For a long time, the Commonwealth was represented at the conferences only by invitation, and the agenda was confined largely to purely state concerns, with only an occasional matter involving interstate interests. The financial distresses of the twenties

[1] Davies, *Australian Democracy*, p. 99.

turned the states toward Canberra, however, and after the creation of the Loan Council by the Financial Agreement of 1927, the conferences came more and more under federal leadership, as reflected in their present official title, Conferences of Commonwealth and State Ministers. It is not without meaning that the Commonwealth precedes the states. Today the conferences provide opportunity for the premiers to discuss interstate interests, as they have all along, but they are now convened on Commonwealth initiative—and are held more often than not in Canberra—and the first items on their agenda are usually matters of Commonwealth interest on which the Prime Minister wants advice and counsel.

Although the Premiers' Conferences are important interstate meetings, involving as they do the men who are the dominant political figures in the states, it is not necessary to discuss them at great length here. They are one of the few exceptions to the rule that interstate relations have been ignored in Australian literature on government. They have been described in a number of places,[2] perhaps because their meetings (and those of the Australian Loan Council, which since its inception has had virtually the same membership and meets normally in conjunction with the Premiers' Conferences) have always made headlines. Only a few general comments will therefore suffice.

It should be remembered first of all that the Premiers' Conferences are more concerned with Commonwealth-state relations than they are with interstate relations. On the one hand they provide a "convenient occasion for the Commonwealth to seek to influence state policies,"[3] and on the other

[2] See for example K. N. J. Bernie, "The Premiers' Conferences. An Historical Sketch from the Beginnings to 1930," *Public Administration*, VII (December 1947), 410–17; A. J. A. Gardner, "Commonwealth-State Administrative Relations," in Spann (ed.), *Public Administration in Australia*, pp. 234–57.
[3] Davies, "Victorian Government and Politics," p. 287.

they serve the states as a counterpoise against the Commonwealth. Professor Miller, indeed, concluded that the premiers "come to Canberra to look for money and to discuss the effects of Federal policy" on state autonomy and suggested that the conferences' chief utility is that they provide a place where the clash between federal demands and state resistance to them can be fought out peacefully.[4] All this is quite true. The conferences are nevertheless important from the interstate point of view for at least three reasons. The virtual merger of the Premiers' Conference and the Australian Loan Council has assured the states of a regular opportunity to get together for discussion at the highest policy level. Because of its membership and the breadth of its agenda,[5] the Premiers' Conference is perhaps the only place where any and all aspects of state governmental activity can be brought up for

[4] Miller, *Australian Government and Politics*, p. 138.

[5] The 1952 meeting of the Premiers' Conference, held in Canberra July 7–8, was typical. Its agenda was as follows:
1. Commonwealth-state financial relations, 1952–1953
2. Petrol tax allocations—Commonwealth-aid roads
3. Financing Commonwealth activities undertaken by the states
4. Retarding of soldier settlement schemes due to difficulties in loan financing
5. Local government finances
6. Loan funds
7. Import licenses for state governments
8. Schools in military camps and migrant hostels
9. Commonwealth financial assistance toward costs of university education
10. Administration of Commonwealth scholarship scheme
11. Income tax deductions for teacher training bursars
12. Financial provisions for school buildings
13. Employment by the Commonwealth of teachers trained by the states before completion of bonded period
14. Hospital finances
15. Mental hospital benefits
16. Red Cross blood transfusion service
17. Maternal and child hygiene
18. Means of encouraging tobacco production in Australia
19. Shortage of men for maintenance of railway stock
20. Uniform company law
21. Use on highways in Victoria of Commonwealth vehicles
22. Children's literature

discussion. And finally, because of the nature of the Australian political system, those who attend the meetings are always the leaders of the majority party in their respective states and are thus in a position to implement conference recommendations at home, when it is necessary.

Some mention might be made in the second place of the meetings themselves. Usually the Premiers' Conferences meet in conjunction with the Australian Loan Council, which was created to control and regulate the borrowings of both the Commonwealth and the state governments; governmental budgets being what they are, the council must meet at least once a year to get its business done. As its membership is practically identical to that of the Premiers' Conference,[6] and as satisfactory meeting times for men as busy as premiers and state treasurers are hard to arrange across six state lines, it is often convenient for the two sessions to be telescoped into one. Normally, the meetings of the council

[6] The representatives of the governments at the July 15, 1961, meeting of the Premiers' Conference were as follows:

Commonwealth:	The Prime Minister, Mr. Menzies
	The Treasurer, Mr. Holt
	The Minister for Health, Mr. Cameron
New South Wales:	The Premier, Mr. Heffron
Victoria:	The Premier and Treasurer, Mr. Bolte
	The Chief Secretary and Attorney General, Mr. Rylah
Queensland:	The Premier and Chief Secretary, Mr. Nicklin
	The Treasurer, Mr. Hiley
South Australia:	The Premier and Treasurer, Sir Thomas Playford
Western Australia:	The Premier and Treasurer, Mr. Brand
Tasmania:	The Premier and Treasurer, Mr. Reece

The Commonwealth *Directory* listed the members of the Australian Loan Council as of July 1961 as follows:

Commonwealth:	The Treasurer, Mr. Holt
New South Wales:	The Premier, Mr. Heffron
Victoria:	The Premier and Treasurer, Mr. Bolte
Queensland:	The Premier, Mr. Nicklin
South Australia:	The Premier and Treasurer, Sir Thomas Playford
Western Australia:	The Premier and Treasurer, Mr. Brand
Tasmania:	The Premier, Mr. Reece

(Commonwealth of Australia, *Directory to . . . Departments and Authorities* [Canberra, 1961], p. 89.)

are called when it suits the Commonwealth to hold them. By custom, however, if the premiers of three states want a meeting and one has not been called by the chairman of the council (who is the Commonwealth Treasurer in name, the Prime Minister in fact), they may request him to call one, and he must comply. And of course other meetings of the conference are held from time to time.

Once the meeting is under way, the Commonwealth has a rather free hand in running it. The meetings are now almost always held in Canberra, and the premiers are thus all in a sense guests of the Commonwealth government and so subject to the behavior patterns which that implies. A good deal depends on the Prime Minister. Sir Thomas Playford, who has attended more Premiers' Conferences than anyone else in Australia as a consequence of his long tenure as premier of South Australia, likened the meetings of the conference in Prime Minister Joseph B. Chifley's day to the story about President Lincoln's cabinet meeting—"Noes seven, ayes one. The ayes have it."[7] Certainly the tradition has developed that the Prime Minister presides and that he runs the meetings, if not in accordance with his own inclinations, at least from the Commonwealth point of view. The flavor of the meetings is caught in the final exchange between the Prime Minister and the premier of New South Wales at the June 15, 1961, meeting of the Conference:

"Mr. MENZIES: I think that concludes our business, and I thank you for your attendance.

"Mr. HEFFRON: Might I, Mr. Prime Minister, on behalf of the Premiers, thank you very much for presiding at our meeting, and for the gracious and sympathetic hearing you have given us. We shall go away in the hope that something will come out of the meeting. I would like to thank you also for

[7] Interview with Sir Thomas Playford, Adelaide, Australia, November 1, 1961.

the hospitality that you always accord us when we come to Canberra."[8]

To the degree that the Prime Minister uses Premiers' Conferences merely as a sounding board for Commonwealth proposals or limits the discussion to items of his choice, their value in terms of interstate relations is obviously reduced. But even a Prime Minister hostile to interstate cooperation —and there is no indication that there have been any—could not avoid presenting at least some opportunities for interstate questions to be raised. Governmental borrowing is inextricably bound up with the whole problem of government finances—and thus of government in general—so that every conference-council meeting offers some occasion for discussion to move in the direction of interstate relations. And a number of financial items of course are directly concerned with intergovernmental cooperation, and if they usually involve Commonwealth-state relations, the lessons they provide for interstate relations are not lost on the premiers. Even at the meetings of the conference apart from the council, which have usually been called by the Prime Minister—or occasionally by the state premiers—to deal with one topic only, or several related ones, and which seldom last longer than one day, the conversation will sometimes stray to interstate problems. Every now and then, an item directly concerned with interstate cooperation is listed on the agenda, as was the question of uniform company law at the conferences of 1946 and 1952.[9] Sometimes such items are referred to the premiers from outside. Their discussion in 1948 of a tuberculosis campaign is a good example. Tuberculosis had long been a serious problem in Australia. Prior to World War II, there had been a great deal of inconclusive

[8] Commonwealth of Australia, *Conference of Commonwealth and State Ministers . . . 15th June, 1961, Proceedings of the Conference* (Canberra, 1961), p. 13.

[9] See p. 140 below.

discussion about how to attack it, but no firm decisions had been reached. After the war, the problem was taken up again. This time the Commonwealth Minister for Health appointed a specialist, Sir Harry Wunderly, to make an investigation and report back to him. On the basis of Wunderly's report, delivered in November 1947, the minister called a conference of state and federal health officers to develop a plan of action. This group prepared a plan that it submitted to another conference, this time of state and Commonwealth ministers of health, in June 1948, which conference adopted it and in turn recommended it to the Premiers' Conference scheduled for August 1948. That conference took it up as agenda item number one and unanimously resolved at the conclusion of its discussion that a cooperative antituberculosis campaign be undertaken at once. Similarly, at the Premiers' Conference in February 1962, consideration was given to a statement prepared and submitted by the Australian Education Council concerning certain deficiencies in Australian education.

But all these possibilities for considering interstate cooperation notwithstanding, time and a surfeit of important problems of government that must be discussed prevent the Premiers' Conferences from devoting much of their energy in formal sessions to the nurture of interstate cooperation. Two days is the average length of their meetings—and there are seldom more than two meetings a year—and a look back at the agenda for the July 1952 conference, which was a typical session, reminds us how much ground the conference attempts to cover in that short length of time.[10]

It is not necessary, however, for official attention to be devoted to interstate relations at the Premiers' Conferences to make them valuable arenas for the development of interstate cooperation. Far more important than formal discussion

[10] See note 5, *supra*.

for that development are the informal contacts that take place at every conference between premiers and their ministers. In the halls and hotel lobbies, over the luncheon table and during conference breaks, these key state officials—already likely bound together by a common stand they have taken against the Commonwealth—share their experiences and compare notes. The premiers are almost always accompanied to the meetings by two or three other key ministers in their governments. Where the premier is not also the treasurer, the latter will be sure to come. The public service commissioner often makes a third member of the team, and once in a while, a premier will bring a rising junior minister along with him as well. All these lesser lights join the premiers in exchanging information with one another, in describing their problems to each other, and in asking for suggestions for solving them. In the course of their conversations, they often see chances for cooperative action, and when they return home, more likely than not they will set the necessary wheels in motion. None of the actions taken at a Premiers' Conference, either after formal discussion by resolution or after informal consideration in the halls and corridors, are binding on the participating governments. Each retains complete freedom of action. But the conferences have acquired enough prestige, and they are well enough reported in the press, that both the formal agreements and the informal commitments reached there have a good chance of being acted upon back home. This is not always a tangible thing; sometimes, indeed, nothing specific is actually articulated. But all the state representatives at Premiers' Conferences whom I interviewed in Australia agreed that the atmosphere at those meetings conduces to cooperation and that they must be acknowledged as a prime force in bringing about the degree of thinking in interstate terms that has come to exist in Australia. Although there are obviously party and personality differences which sometimes stand in the way of cooperation after the conference is over, it is remarkable how good the states' record is in working together in new ways after virtually every Premiers' Conference. Even when a state remains aloof, unanimity among the other states at least warns it of the way the wind is blowing and suggests that it cannot long hold up something the other states want.

Other Conferences Develop

As the depression and then the accumulation of postwar needs multiplied the number of problems that had to be faced, it became clear that the Premiers' Conferences were not enough by themselves to provide the Commonwealth with the kind of advice and counsel it needed in a number of important areas of action. They had the double disadvantage of meeting relatively infrequently and of not being able to dig very deeply into any particular problem or group of problems when they did meet. Consequently, the habit gradually developed of holding supplemental meetings at the ministerial and departmental levels on the model of the Premiers' Conference. Indeed, the latter's chief importance may turn out to be the example it has provided the Commonwealth and the states in setting up a number of what might be called "area conferences." Today, there are nearly a dozen Commonwealth-state groups in nearly as many fields, which, like the Premiers' Conferences, are part of the federal government's machinery but which incidentally make a significant contribution to the development of interstate relations. Listed alphabetically, they are:

> Australian Agricultural Council
> Australian Apprenticeship Advisory Committee
> Australian Transport Advisory Council
> Commonwealth-States Committee on Exchange
>   of Information on Atomic Energy

Commonwealth-States Committee on Safety
in Industrial Atomic Energy
Conferences of Federal and State Fisheries
Ministers and Officers
Departments of Labour Advisory Committee
National Health and Medical Research Council
National Mapping Council
National Tuberculosis Advisory Committee

The Commonwealth Art Advisory Board might be included in the list inasmuch as a by-product of its work is to get state art galleries to cooperate with one another in lending pictures, holding exhibitions, and so on. Some of these groups have broader concerns than others; some are older and better established. All of them are convened on Commonwealth initiative and exist primarily to present state officers with opportunities to discuss and advise on matters of Commonwealth interest. All of them, however, provide occasions for purely state matters to be discussed as well, for personal contacts to be made or strengthened, and for plans and programs to be shared between state officials. It is out of such things that interstate cooperation grows. Some conference discussions, moreover, result in recommendations for interstate cooperation being made to the states. Like the Premiers' Conference, none of the lesser conferences is endowed with power to act independently of the participating governments, but since each conference involves the persons most directly responsible for securing state action in that particular field of activity, recommendations have a good chance of being adopted by the states.

Australian Agricultural Council

The oldest of these Commonwealth advisory groups, and next to the Premiers' Conference, the prototype for most of the others, is the Australian Agricultural Council.[11] It had its origin in a conference of state ministers of agriculture and ministers of appropriate Commonwealth departments on agricultural production and marketing matters in 1934. Its value was quickly recognized, and it soon became a permanent and rather elaborate organization whose many contributions to the growth of Australia's agricultural potential have been generally acknowledged. Today it consists of the Commonwealth Minister for Primary Industry as chairman, the Commonwealth Ministers for Trade and for Territories, and the ministers of agriculture of the six states. It generally meets twice a year, its fifty-seventh meeting having been held in July 1962.[12] For a long time now, it has met in a pattern of rotation at the various capital cities. Although the official version of its purpose is described as being "to provide a basis for continuous consultation amongst Australian governments on economic aspects of primary production and marketing of primary products,"[13] the council in fact ranges widely over all aspects of Australian agriculture, including research, extension, and administration. Its manifold interests are served by a secretary supplied by the Department of Primary Industry. It is advised by a permanent Standing Committee on Agriculture, which consists of the head officers of the state departments of agriculture and representatives of a number of Commonwealth departments, including the Treasury, the Department of Health, the Department of Territories, the Department of Trade, and the Commonwealth Scientific and Industrial Research Organisation. Unlike the chairmanship of the council itself, the chairmanship of the standing com-

[11] See F. O. Grogan, "The Australian Agricultural Council: Successful Experiment in Commonwealth-State Relations," *Public Administration*, XVII (March 1958), 1–21; see also Gardner, "Commonwealth-State Relations," pp. 240–41.
[12] For a report of that meeting, see *Australia in Facts and Figures*, No. 75 (September quarter 1962), pp. 72–75.
[13] The phraseology used in Commonwealth *Directory*, p. 27.

mittee is rotated among the states. Ordinarily, meetings of the committee precede meetings of the council—although the committee meets at other times as well—and a large part of the council's agenda is composed of committee submissions. The normal procedure is for the states to suggest items for the committee's consideration. The committee then screens them and handles them in one of two ways. If the matter requires a policy decision, it is placed on the council's agenda at once; if the matter is a technical one, the committee is apt to refer it to a subcommittee for investigation and ask it to report its findings back to the committee at a later date. The committee is advised in turn by a number of technical committees and subcommittees, such as the Animal Production Committee, the Sub-Committee on Beef Research Proposals, the Australian Seed Campaign Committee, the Technical Committee on Storage of Seeds in the Tropics, and the Wheat Quality and Grading Committee. There is also a Standing Committee on Soil Conservation, which passes its recommendations through the Standing Committee on Agriculture to the council. This is a Commonwealth-wide body that meets annually and limits its discussions to matters in the conservation area. In addition to the services performed for it by these committees, the council has the power to co-opt the services of Commonwealth and state departments and officers as required. The decisions reached by the council on the basis of all the evidence submitted to it take the form of recommendations to the appropriate state and federal government departments.

Apart from its study and recommendatory functions, the council concerns itself with coordinating a wide range of activities, such as organizing national scientific conferences like the conference on soil science, which brought forty people from a wide variety of federal and state agencies and private industry to Canberra in February 1961, for example; sponsoring university scholarships; arranging tours for overseas study;

and conducting a number of informational and advisory services. In recent years a number of the primary industries, including wheat, tobacco, barley, and dairying, have imposed a levy on their own producers for the purpose of developing research and extension programs. The Commonwealth government and the states too have contributed funds, and the council administers the funds as a special service.

In its activities, the Agricultural Council serves the cause of interstate cooperation in a number of ways. Its meetings, and those of the two standing committees and of their subcommittees as well, provide opportunities for the mutual exchange of information regarding agricultural production and marketing among the several Australian governments. The New South Wales Department of Agriculture, for example, commented enthusiastically in a report in 1959 on the "interchange of information and material between itself and other state departments of agriculture" and mentioned in particular the value derived from the exchange of up-to-date production data and other marketing matters.[14] The meetings also provide occasions for representatives of state departments to consult together and thus avoid unnecessary overlapping and duplication of efforts. And since the meetings of the council are held successively in different state capitals, those concerned with a particular kind of program in one state have opportunities to see for themselves what their counterparts in other states are doing and where their own programs might be coordinated with others.

In addition to their responsibilities to the Commonwealth government, both the council and its subordinate committees work directly to secure cooperation and coordination in the

[14] Department of Agriculture, New South Wales, "Notes on the Relationship of Commonwealth, State and Overseas Government and Non-Government Organisations to the Department of Agriculture" (mimeographed report, 1959), p. 50. The entire report is worth careful reading, for it is almost the only extant government-issued material that deals specifically with intergovernmental relations.

initiation and conduct of agricultural research and in the development of agricultural regulations, particularly those relating to quarantine, among the state governments. As a result of council leadership, a number of cooperative research projects have been undertaken between state departments of agriculture on the one hand and the Commonwealth Scientific and Industrial Research Organisation on the other, among them projects relating to commodity treatments for fruit fly and a trial campaign for grasshopper eradication. The council is responsible too for the fact that today the agricultural seeds acts of all the states are relatively uniform and the certification requirements for seed are virtually the same in all the states. Similarly, it was through the council's agency that reciprocal arrangements with regard to the introduction of certain fruits, plants, and vegetables into the states were developed. The council persuaded the states to cooperate in the first place in passing complementary legislation establishing production quotas for table margarine, and in 1962 held a conference of legal and technical officers from all the states, which resolved that the states should now switch instead to uniform legislation respecting margarine.[15] Finally, as a result of council discussions, the states have agreed to permit the Commonwealth to do all their meat inspection for them, to avoid the duplication and conflict that formerly marked that area of activity. Indeed, there is close cooperation today between the states in all areas of agriculture, and it is due largely, Australian state officials are frank to admit, to the harmony induced by the council's operation over the years.

Fisheries Council

The pattern set by the Agricultural Council has recently been followed in the field of fisheries with the creation of a

15 See *Australia in Facts and Figures,* No. 75, p. 75; see also p. 101.

conference of Commonwealth and state fisheries ministers and with the formalization of a conference of federal-state fisheries officers.[16] Representatives of state fisheries departments had been coming together from time to time for some years, and in 1955, since fisheries had assumed an important place in the Australian economy, they began to meet annually. They decided very quickly, however, that they could not get very far alone because every question involving policy matters had to be referred back to the ministers in the several states and sometimes to the Commonwealth government in Canberra as well. In 1958, the departmental officers began to press for a ministers' council modeled after the Agricultural Council, and in 1960, after a meeting of ministers called by the Commonwealth government to discuss the proposal, such a body was established. It is to function in the same way as the Agricultural Council does and will provide the same kind of opportunities for interstate cooperation in fisheries as the Agricultural Council provides in the agricultural field.

Like their agricultural counterparts, the two fisheries groups are concerned with advising the Commonwealth and state governments on questions of fisheries production and management and with promoting the welfare of the Australian fisheries industry. Their methods of approach will include the mutual exchange of information on various aspects of fisheries, cooperative efforts both to improve the quality of their products and to develop and maintain high-grade standards in the industry, development of uniform policies for management and overseas marketing, and coordination of state laws

[16] "There is still some indecision about the formal title of the Inter-State/Federal Fisheries Conference and for the moment it would appear that [it] will in future be known as 'The Conference of Federal and States Fisheries Officers' . . . [the] Conference of Commonwealth and States Fisheries Ministers . . . when necessary, will follow a Conference of Officers." A. Dunbavin Butcher, Director of Fisheries and Wildlife, State of Victoria, to author, November 19, 1962. Eventually, the same nomenclature used in connection with the agricultural bodies—council and standing committee—will probably be adopted.

controlling adjacent ocean fisheries.[17] The chairman of the ministers' conference will be the Commonwealth Minister for Primary Industry, and a secretary will be provided from the same department. In every important detail both the ministers' group and the officers' group plan to follow the usages of the Agricultural Council. Already a number of cooperative projects have been launched under the aegis of the two groups, including an annual Australian Fisheries School for field officers, the Southern Pelagic Project, which involves the four southern states and two Commonwealth departments, and discussions between the same four states leading to uniform management of the crayfish industry. At the September 1962 meeting of the conferences in Sydney, a resolution calling for the states to cooperate in the passage of legislation for the control and elimination of noxious fish was adopted, and within two months, Victoria had acted on the recommendation, and bills were being prepared to deal with the matter in the other states. Within a very few years, the fisheries group will probably be making as significant a contribution to interstate cooperation in its area of concern as the Agricultural Council has been making in its own for over a quarter of a century.

National Health and Medical Research Council

Almost as venerable a body as the Agricultural Council is the National Health and Medical Research Council. The Commonwealth first created an advisory body in the field of health in 1926, when it established the Federal Health Council. In 1936, however, the Commonwealth decided broader functions and representation were needed, and the next year the National Health and Medical Research Council was

[17] *Australia in Facts and Figures*, No. 71 (September quarter 1961), p. 71; see also Department of Primary Industry, Commonwealth Director of Fisheries, *Fisheries Newsletter*, XIX (January 1960), p. 7.

brought into being.[18] It consists of the Commonwealth Director General of Health as chairman and three officers of the Commonwealth Department of Health, appointed by the Health Minister, the state directors general of health, twelve other members nominated from the various professional medical and dental associations, and two lay members. The chief functions of the council are to inquire into and to advise the Commonwealth and state governments on matters of public health legislation and administration and on any matters concerning public health, medical and dental care, and medical research that it thinks warrant government attention. It also advises the governments on the merits of reputed cures or methods of treatment that are brought forward from time to time, and since 1938 it has been charged with giving the Commonwealth advice concerning federal expenditures on medical research. The council usually meets twice a year in Canberra and is provided with a secretariat by the Commonwealth Department of Health. It has appointed a number of committees of outside experts to assist it, and the general opinion is that these committees have made an important contribution to the improvement of public health practices in Australia.[19]

The council's meetings provide opportunities for interstate cooperation to be discussed, and a great many of the council's resolutions deal with cooperation and uniformity among the states. At the fiftieth session of the council, held in Canberra in October 1960, for example, seven of the thirteen resolutions passed were wholly or in part concerned with cooperative state action. Among them were recommendations urging the states to adopt and use a uniform form of notification of the occurrence of venereal disease and a uniform medical record

[18] Commonwealth Bureau of Census and Statistics, *Year Book of the Commonwealth of Australia*, No. 44 (1958), p. 528.
[19] For a description of the committees' work, see the annual *Report of the Director-General of Health*.

of birth.[20] Through the years, the states for their part have built up an admirable record of accepting the council's recommendations.

National Tuberculosis Advisory Council

Another advisory body in the field of health is the National Tuberculosis Advisory Council, which consists of the Commonwealth and state officers concerned with tuberculosis control and the purpose of which is to advise the Commonwealth Minister for Health on matters relating to that effort. Both in the way it goes about its work and in the opportunities it creates for interstate cooperation it is very like the National Health and Medical Research Council.

Departments of Labour Advisory Committee

The Departments of Labour Advisory Committee had its genesis in one of a number of resolutions adopted by a Conference of Commonwealth and State Ministers for Labour convened in 1947 to consider some of the then current problems in the field. The resolution read in part: "The Conference resolves that the question of standards throughout the Commonwealth should be kept under constant review and periodical conferences of officers of the State Departments of Labour [should] be convened by the Commonwealth Department of Labour and National Service to discuss and review such standards with a view to submitting recommendations . . . for consideration."[21] The Commonwealth very shortly thereafter called the first such conference,

[20] Commonwealth of Australia, Report of the National Health and Medical Research Council, Fiftieth Session Held at Canberra, 27th October, 1960 (Canberra, 1960), pp. 37–38.

[21] A copy of the resolution was very kindly supplied me by the Department of Labour and Industry of Victoria, as was most of the information that I have used here on the Departments of Labour Advisory Committee.

and all the states were represented except Queensland. Among other things it was decided at that first meeting that the title "Departments of Labour Advisory Committee" be adopted for the group and that meetings should be held at intervals of not more than six months; that a review should be made of industrial welfare standards then in force and of desirable standards in the field for adoption by the states; that the relevant research should be carried on by the Commonwealth Department of Labour and National Service; and that a conspectus of state legislation and awards on physical working conditions be drawn up and kept up to date by the Commonwealth Department. After that meeting, the committee met three more times. A fifth meeting was scheduled for October 1949, but in the interim two of the state departments of labor withdrew from the committee because of dissatisfaction with proposed arrangements for the coordination of the work of the Commonwealth and state factory inspectorates. The work of the committee then lapsed.

Even during that short period, however, the committee—already called DOLAC for short—accomplished a good deal. It provided for the first time an opportunity for regular meetings between state labor people; before DOLAC began to meet, the permanent head of the labour department in one state might not even have known the names of his counterparts in the other states, much less have had contact with them. It also was responsible for the adoption by all the participating departments of a number of standards of physical working conditions, known as DOLAC Recommended Standards. They included such subjects as dining rooms, change rooms and restrooms, sanitary and washing accommodations, working conditions in foundries, removal of dust, smoke, and fumes, and natural lighting in offices. In addition, a mutually beneficial exchange of information was inaugurated.

By 1955, concern had been expressed both by the Commonwealth and by several of the states about the growing lack of coordination between the many organizations, governmental and otherwise, that dealt with various aspects of industrial safety, and it was suggested that DOLAC be revived to develop and coordinate programs devoted to industrial accident prevention. The Commonwealth passed the suggestion along to the state departments of labor, and there was general acceptance of the idea by all the states, including Queensland. As a consequence, DOLAC met twice in 1955, and has met yearly since then. One of the first matters to which the reconstituted committee gave attention was the planning of an Australia-wide industrial safety campaign. Arising out of its efforts was the National Conference on Industrial Safety held in Canberra in September 1958. Since then safety conventions have been organized, with the committee's help, in most of the states. DOLAC resumed its work on the development of recommended standards for physical working conditions, and a half dozen or more have been adopted by the states. Much useful work has also been done in resolving conflicts between state awards legislation.

Although its first loyalty, so to speak, is to the Commonwealth and although its major concern is to help work out problems of competition arising between Commonwealth and state programs in the labor field, DOLAC gives every promise of bringing the states into a still closer working relationship, at least in the areas of industrial safety and working standards. The difficulties between the states and the Commonwealth over factory inspection, which caused suspension earlier, have been overcome, and all the states are now giving the committee their full cooperation. It was agreed at the meeting in 1961 that each department would put every other department on its mailing list to receive copies of all acts, amendments to acts, regulations, and instructions that it issued. With such an exchange of information, and with regular occasions through meetings of DOLAC for individuals to meet and compare notes, further examples of cooperation among state labor people will surely be forthcoming.

Australian Apprenticeship Advisory Committee

The other labor advisory body is the Australian Apprenticeship Advisory Committee, which stems from a recommendation of a special Federal-State Committee of Enquiry into Apprenticeship in Australia after World War II.[22] Until that time, an almost medieval system of apprenticeship was still in effect in a number of Australian states, and the changing times demanded drastic action if training methods were to be improved. Inasmuch as apprenticeship and technical training are, broadly speaking, matters within the jurisdiction of the states, the Commonwealth decided to establish liaison with state apprenticeship and technical education authorities and thus, in the guise of seeking their advice, to lead them toward far-reaching remedial programs. To that end, it constituted the Australian Apprenticeship Advisory Committee, which held its first meeting in February 1957. Since then it has met annually. As is the case with DOLAC, the Commonwealth Department of Labour and National Service provides the committee with a secretariat. The committee itself consists of officers concerned with apprenticeship and technical training in the states, along with representatives of the Commonwealth department. Meeting on the basis of mutual consultation, taking no votes but endeavoring to reach agreement, the committee has worked in a number of areas, including: the design of apprenticeship curricula and post-apprenticeship courses in the light of changing techniques of industry; the improvement and standardization of statistics in the apprenticeship and technical training fields; methods of systematic selection of apprentices; the conduct of basic

[22] *Australia in Facts and Figures,* No. 46 (June quarter 1955), p. 56.

research into matters affecting apprenticeship; and the dissemination of ideas, information, and laws concerning all aspects of apprenticeship throughout the Commonwealth. In all these areas, the Apprenticeship Advisory Committee has served to bring state people together and thus as a catalyst for a good deal of cooperation and coordination among them.

National Mapping Council

Two other bodies advisory to the Commonwealth ought to be mentioned, the National Mapping Council and the Australian Transport Advisory Council. The National Mapping Council is composed of the Commonwealth Director of National Mapping, the Director of Army Survey, the Chief Hydrographic Officer of the Navy, and the Commonwealth Surveyor General as Commonwealth members and the state surveyors general, who are responsible for mapping in the states, from the states. The council is advisory to the Minister for National Development and its primary concern is to serve as the agency for coordinating all the mapping and surveying programs in Australia. Meeting annually since 1945, the council has discussed virtually every aspect of the problem and has passed a number of resolutions which accept intergovernmental cooperation as the norm in mapping and surveying activities. Thus one resolution, for example, recommends that when geodetic survey, aerial photography, or mapping are contemplated by one state in an area adjoining a state boundary, the possibilities of a joint operation with the adjoining state or states be investigated.[23] Acting on that recommendation, New South Wales has cooperated with both Queensland and Victoria in aerial photography. In addition to meetings of the council itself, formal relations in

[23] Report of the Department of Lands, New South Wales, to the Under Secretary, Premier's Department, Fall, 1960. G. Gray, Under Secretary, Premier's Department, to author, November 2, 1960.

such technical fields as photogrammetry and cartography are maintained between the states through the Technical Sub-Committee of the council, on which each member of the council is represented. The subcommittee meets yearly, usually in advance of the council, and ensures the exchange of information and advice on technical operations between the persons concerned. Since the council began to function, mapping has become an integrated operation in Australia, and at the council's urging, cooperation between the states has marked every step of the way.[24]

Australian Transport Advisory Council

Perhaps the Australian Transport Advisory Council has been more productive of interstate cooperation than any of the other advisory groups with the sole exception of the Agricultural Council. Under the Commonwealth Constitution, responsibility for transportation is divided between the Commonwealth and the states, the Commonwealth being responsible for transport administration and road construction in the territories and for interstate shipping, civil aviation, and the Commonwealth railways, whereas the states are responsible for the state railway systems, road construction and maintenance, ports and harbors, and intrastate transport regulation. Obviously, a coordinating device was badly needed, particularly when the continent came to life again after World War II. In 1946, the Transport Advisory Council was created to fill the need. It consists of the Commonwealth Minister for Shipping and Transport as chairman, the Ministers for National Development, Interior, Army, and Territories, and each state minister for transport. As it does for the other advisory commissions, the Commonwealth provides the council with a staff. The council meets once a year in the normal

[24] For a full discussion of mapping and surveys in Australia, see *Australia in Facts and Figures*, No. 65 (March quarter 1960), pp. 37–48.

course of events—more often when necessary[25]—to discuss transport generally and road transport in particular, together with problems of transport regulation and road safety. It is particularly charged with recommending steps "which will tend to promote a better co-ordination of transport development" in Australia.[26] The council has no powers of itself, and its importance lies in the exchange of views it makes possible and in the recommendations it makes to the states for uniform action. The council early created subcommittees, of which there are now five. Three of them are specially directed towards achieving uniform state action.[27] The Australian Road Traffic Code Committee, which is composed of representatives from the various state government departments connected with road traffic, the Commonwealth government, and a number of national organizations concerned with transport,[28] is responsible for recommendations leading to uniformity in the traffic laws of the several states. A model traffic code has been prepared by the committee and submitted to the council. At the council's twentieth meeting in 1962, it was discussed and endorsed in principle. Although it was recognized that the code might "not necessarily be adopted in all States, [the council] expressed the hope that each State would, as opportunity offered, adopt the provisions of the code."[29] The code covers such things as speed limits,

[25] The council's twentieth meeting was held in June 1962. For the first time, it met in Darwin.

[26] Department of Shipping and Transport, "The Australian Transport Advisory Council and its Main Committees" (mimeographed report, 1958), p. 2; see also D. C. L. Williams, "The Role of the Commonwealth in Land and Sea Transport," *Public Administration*, XVIII (June 1959), 192–93.

[27] The two subcommittees that are not so directly concerned with fostering uniform state action are the Australian Road Safety Council, which is an educational body, and the Committee of Transport Economic Research, whose interests are explained by its title.

[28] The Australian Automobile Association, the Australian Road Transport Federation, the Associated Chambers of Commerce, and the Transport Workers' Union of Australia.

[29] *Australia in Facts and Figures*, No. 74 (June quarter 1962), p. 107.

right-hand turn rules, rules governing approaches to inter-
sections, qualifications of drivers, and pedestrian behavior.
To date, state reaction has been favorable, and a high degree
of uniformity among the states promises eventually to be
achieved. The Australian Motor Vehicles Standards Committee is composed of representatives of the agencies administering transport both in the states and in the Commonwealth and of organizations of motor vehicle manufacturers
and operators. As is the case with the Road Traffic Code
Committee, its chairman is a representative of the Commonwealth Department of Shipping and Transport. Its activities
are aimed at bringing about uniformity in the requirements
of each state concerning motor vehicle standards. Standards
with regard to lighting, reflectors, trailer couplings, mud-
guards, and performance ability of brakes, tires, and emergency exits have already been developed and approved by
the council, and the states have begun to adopt them. A
number of other standards are in the process of development.
In 1960, for example, a Dangerous Goods Transport Committee was appointed to study the need for uniformity of
regulations concerning the transportation of explosives. The
committee reported back to the council in 1963 and began
to prepare a set of model regulations.

The council also works closely with the National Association of Australian State Road Authorities, which represents
the road building authorities in the states. Early in its operations the council accepted as the standard for the Australian
road system the road and bridge design standards developed
by the association, and recommended them to the states. As
a result, road construction throughout the Commonwealth
has become more uniform. On occasion, the council convenes
special conferences of persons in state road agencies. In recent
years, such conferences have examined highway planning,
accidents at railway crossings, accidents involving motor-
cyclists, and problems of pedestrian behavior.

With the rapid development of Australian road transport in recent years, a number of new areas of action have been suggested to the council. At its June 1962 meeting, for example, the council's chairman, H. F. Opperman, the Federal Minister for Shipping and Transport, announced that "uniformity in the field of the liability of carriers by air was becoming of vital importance," and that "the desirability and practicability of uniform liability of carriers by road transport" should also be investigated.[30] A committee to look into both matters and report back to the council was subsequently appointed. Other possibilities for future council action include uniform regulations for hours of driving in interstate transport, standardization of large freight containers, and joint action to solve the problems created by the effect of Section 92 of the Constitution on road transport, as far as the equitable assignment of road use charges for interstate carriers is concerned.[31]

Ad Hoc Commonwealth Conferences

In addition to the advisory bodies that have become regular parts of the governmental machinery, the Commonwealth also brings representatives of the states together from time to time in various ad hoc conferences and committees. The conferences on weights and measures are a case in point. Under the Australian Constitution, the Commonwealth is endowed with power to make laws dealing with weights and measures, and in 1948 it exercised this power by passing the Weights and Measures (National Standards) Act. This act was intended to establish a uniform system of weights and measures throughout the Commonwealth and to provide for

[30] *Ibid.*, p. 106.
[31] See the reports of meetings and activities of the council, *ibid.*, No. 57 (March quarter 1958), p. 73; No. 66 (June quarter 1960), p. 86; No. 69, p. 72; and No. 74, p. 107.

all the states to have their standards periodically verified by comparison with Commonwealth standards. A number of difficulties, largely legal, arose as the act was implemented, and in order to expedite matters, the Commonwealth called three conferences—in 1952, 1958, and 1959—which were attended by representatives of weights and measures administrations in the states. Although the conferences were held primarily to discuss the problems posed by the 1948 act, they also had the result of enabling weights and measures officers from the several states to become acquainted with one another and to discuss extensively other matters of mutual interest. As a result, in the last few years, there has been a substantial exchange of information in regard to kinds of weighing and measuring equipment approved for use in trade in the various states, and officers of the state weights and measures administrations have formed the habit of contacting each other by letter whenever it appears that information regarding practice or intentions in other states would be of assistance. The occasional conferences at both the ministerial and the officer level of state officers concerned with migrant care and the Plant Quarantine Conference of 1960 are other illustrations of Commonwealth ad hoc conferences.

On at least one occasion an ad hoc conference has led to the creation of a permanent advisory body. This was the case with a conference on underground water called in 1959.[32] In recognition of the importance of water resources to the future development of Australia and of the need for coordinated action in their development, the Commonwealth called a conference on underground water in Sydney in 1959. Senior Commonwealth and state officers interested in underground water problems were invited to attend, and the whole question

[32] Five earlier conferences about artesian water had been held at intervals between 1912 and 1928, and in 1939 a conference was held dealing with water supply generally. See Department of the Co-Ordinator General of Public Works, Queensland, *Artesian Water Supplies in Queensland* (Brisbane, 1954), pp. 64–65.

of underground water supply and conservation was raised for discussion. The conference agreed among other things that the problems discussed deserved more than sporadic attention and that a permanent body to coordinate both developmental and conservation efforts in the field should be created. The establishment of such a body was recommended to the Commonwealth and the states, and those governments acted promptly on the recommendation. In May 1961 the first annual meeting of the Underground Water Conference of Australia was convened in Canberra, and the second meeting was held in Adelaide in 1962. The conference consists of two members from each state, one member from each territory, a representative of the Commonwealth Scientific and Industrial Research Organisation, and a representative of the Commonwealth Department of National Development, who serves as chairman. To date, it has directed its efforts toward bringing about cooperation in collecting and collating underground water data and devising methods of standardizing both the terminology and the statistics used in field and laboratory work concerned with underground water. It has also initiated a number of joint regional and special investigations relating to using and conserving underground water and to examining training and research needs in underground water fields.

The conference early discovered, however, the need for the involvement of federal and state ministers in its work, and also for their collaboration in work in the broader field of water resources generally. In July 1962 Prime Minister Menzies, acting in response to both needs, proposed the creation of an Australian Water Resources Council along the lines of the Australian Agricultural Council. "In a letter to each State Premier, Mr. Menzies . . . said that what he had in mind immediately were some arrangements for consultation and collaboration between Federal and State authorities to facilitate the sharing of knowledge, to avoid duplication of effort on similar investigations, and generally to achieve fuller cooperation in research and investigation into subjects of common interest, such as measurement of water resources, seepage, evaporation, biological research and demineralization."[33] As the Prime Minister visualized it, the council would be composed of the responsible federal and state ministers in the field, with the Minister for National Development as chairman. It would be supported by a technical standing committee of officers representing federal and state water interests. Perhaps the Underground Water Conference will be altered to assume this role. All the governments promptly agreed to the Prime Minister's suggestion, and the first meeting of the council was held in 1963.

Although ad hoc conferences ordinarily offer less opportunity for interstate cooperation than more regularized conferences do, they have nevertheless been useful in providing additional occasions for a wide range of state officers to meet one another and thereby perhaps to undertake future joint action. When they lead to a permanent arrangement, as was the case in the field of water resources, their contribution is considerably more impressive.

The other Commonwealth organizations listed early in this chapter all work in a similar fashion. Like those already discussed, they were created by the Commonwealth to consider and advise on problems and policies of concern to the federal government. In performing these functions, all the groups use much the same techniques; in fact, one group has frequently served as the model for the next to be established, and its methods have simply been adopted wholesale. These groups do differ, as might be expected, in the amount of interstate cooperation each generates, a situation which arises not from the underlying methods and purposes but from the different problems and individuals involved in each instance. The initiative for all of them has lain in large measure with the Commonwealth. Very much as in the United States,

[33] *Australia in Facts and Figures,* No. 75, p. 92.

where the federal government has in recent years endorsed interstate cooperation by advocating the use of interstate compacts,[34] so, less directly, the Commonwealth government of Australia has moved in the same direction by creating and supporting Commonwealth-state advisory bodies.

The Commonwealth serves the cause of interstate cooperation finally in one or two minor ways. By facilitating the exchange of information among the states in a number of instances, it enables state officials to learn about activities in other states and so, often, to see possibilities for collaboration in programs. The Commonwealth Office of Education, for example, through the service it provides the states as a clearinghouse for information on guidance and counseling, has opened doors to coordination between the states in that area. In the same way, the Commonwealth Scientific and Industrial Research Organisation serves as a catalyst for interstate action in several fields of interest, as do the Commonwealth Department of Works and the Commonwealth Bureau of Census and Statistics. Moreover, Commonwealth officers move about a good deal in the course of their duties, and as they visit state departments and agencies, they sometimes serve as informal go-betweens in the development of interstate cooperation.

All in all, the Commonwealth's role in the growth of interstate cooperation in Australia has been a sizable one. Without the excuse of a Commonwealth conference to attend, many state officials might well have never left their offices and so been introduced to the possibilities of cooperation. Without Commonwealth pressure for Commonwealth-state cooperation, an agenda item at virtually every conference that the Commonwealth has convened, the other side of the same coin, interstate cooperation, might not have been

[34] See author's "The Status of Interstate Compacts Today," *State Government*, XXXII (Spring 1959), 136.

examined nearly as soon as it was. And without Common-wealth leadership in exploring the possibilities of government action generally in a wide variety of fields, the states might not have seen the advantages of coordination and collabora-tion nearly as quickly or as clearly as they have. Indeed, the federal government has been instrumental in providing the proper climate for the rapid growth of interstate cooperation in Australia. Though not always clearly articulated, the Commonwealth has maintained a steady interest in interstate cooperation and has led the states toward its use by example and precept.

Chapter 4 THE STATES AND
INTERSTATE COOPERATION:
THE CONFERENCE WAY

All the inspiration for interstate cooperation has not come
from Canberra. Another great source has been the score or
more groups of state administrators that have come into
existence largely since World War II in response to the
expanding role of state government generally. There is hardly
a field of state government activity today that does not boast
one or more organizations that give officials involved in them
opportunities to become personally acquainted with their
fellow officers across state lines, to share their ideas and views
as well as information, to learn about what is taking place in
their own area of interest in other states, and to work toward
a degree of uniformity in practice and procedure. Perhaps
the reason that there has been so little formal, legally binding,
interstate action in Australia may be that state officials at all
levels have come to depend on their professional organizations
to maintain contact with one another and so to accomplish
what in the larger context of the United States, for example,
would have to be done more formally.

Organizations of State Officials

No complete list of organizations of state officials exists.
Some of these organizations have taken on no regularly
used name and no formal organization at all; others are well
established and well organized, and their names carry a good
deal of prestige. The formal bodies are easier to learn about

because they usually receive publicity in the press; the less formal groups often keep no record of their meetings and are seldom reported on in any detail at all. Neither type has received any scholarly attention. The following list is as complete as I could make it as of the end of 1961.[1]

> Conference of Directors of Education
> Australia and New Zealand City Transit Conference*
> Conference of Water Supply and Sewerage Engineers
> Conference of Australasian Prison Administrators*
> Australian Port Authorities Association*
> The Electricity Supply Association of Australia†
> Association of Government Printers of Australasia
> Conference of State Housing Ministers and Officers
> State Mining Officers Conference
> National Association of Australian State Road
>   Authorities*
> Interstate Health Education Co-ordination Committee
> Conference of State Health Ministers*
> Conference of State Public Service Commissioners*
> Conference of State Government Insurance Officers
> Australia and New Zealand Railway Commissioners
>   Conference*
> Conference of State Police Commissioners
> Conference of State Milk Boards
> State Soil Conservation Officers Conference
> Conference of State Foresters
> Interstate Bush Fire Conference
> Conference of Ministers of Aboriginal Welfare
> Conference of Directors of State Art Galleries

[1] If a group has not been formalized to the extent of having agreed on a name for itself, I have used the name most commonly employed by the people involved. If no single name enjoys wide acceptance, I have tried to use a descriptive and easily recognizable title.

* Sections meet separately but are not listed apart from the parent body.

† Supplying electricity is on the whole a function of state government in Australia.

Conference of State Auditors-General
Conference of State Directors of Child Welfare
Conference of Inspectors of Explosives
Biennial Interstate Fauna Conference
Australian Water Fowl Council
Conference of Government Omnibus and Tramway
    Operators
Conference of Fire Boards
Association of State Librarians of Australia
Interstate Conference on Nursing
Conference of City Building Surveyors
Conference of State Transport Ministers
Conference of State Veterinarians
Interstate Conference of Pest Control Authorities
Conference of Surveyors Boards of Australia
    and New Zealand
Conference of State Directors of Mental Hygiene

Probably the greatest contribution these groups make to interstate cooperation is at their meetings, for it is there that the personal contacts which pay later dividends in terms of cooperation are chiefly made. Like their Commonwealth-oriented counterparts, none of the groups of state people meet for action, in the sense of establishing and carrying on intergovernmental programs. All of them meet instead primarily as discussion groups, dedicated to bringing common problems out into the open and talking over possible joint solutions to them. The cooperation that results from their deliberations is often not spontaneous. It is more likely to be the product of time and of ripening friendships. Anything concrete in the way of cooperative action is purely voluntary on the part of the states and depends on the degree of rapport established between officials in different states rather than on any force that can be brought to bear on any of the parties. The groups have no power whatsoever except the power of persuasion and of the logic of their recommendations.

Although some groups meet very informally, most of them have developed a fairly standard procedure. Meetings are usually held in a different state capital every time. Thus each state in turn acts as host, and every delegate has a chance to see the several state administrative branches at work. Normally, the official representative of the host state—the minister, department head, or divisional officer—serves as chairman and continues in that office until the time of the next meeting. Prior to each meeting, the several members are invited to submit items for the agenda, which is then prepared by the secretary of the group, if it boasts of such an officer. The conferences that have a regular secretariat can of course develop their agenda on a continuous basis throughout the year. Where secretariats are maintained, the cost of their operation is ordinarily handled in one of two ways—either by the assignment of secretarial duties to an officer of one of the member state departments as a part of his job, or by the support of secretarial services by equal or proportionate contributions from each member of the group. If the conference has no secretary, someone on the staff of the chairman's department will be assigned the task. In any case, after the agenda has been prepared, it is usually circulated to the people who will be attending the meeting. The habit has developed in most conferences of inviting the Commonwealth officers most directly concerned with the group's interest to participate as observers, and as a matter of courtesy they are usually sent a copy of the agenda as well. Sometimes a state representative will prepare a detailed statement on one or more agenda items and forward a copy of it to each of the other members before the meeting. Through this means, the representatives know ahead of time what will be discussed and thus are able to prepare in advance. The meetings themselves almost universally last two or three days, although some range up to a full week. In a good many cases, the meetings are broken up into a number of concurrent sessions, so that in large groups, especially, the officers with particular interests are brought together for discussion of their own specialties. The Conference of State Government Insurance Officers thus meets in seven sections—administration, fire, accident, motor vehicle, life, marine, and workmen's compensation; the Electricity Supply Association is organized into five sections—generation, transmission and distribution, accounting and office systems, commercial development and public relations, and personnel and welfare; and the Australia and New Zealand City Transit Conference meets in four divisions—general managers, engineers, traffic officers, and industrial officers. Instead of holding concurrent sessions, a few conferences deal with only certain topics one year, others the next. The Conference of Water Supply and Sewerage Engineers, for example, deals with engineering matters one year, administrative matters the next.

During the session, depending on the custom of the individual group, discussion may be completely off the record and closed to outsiders. In other cases, detailed minutes may be kept. Sometimes resolutions are made at the end of the conference, sometimes they are not. Quite a few groups compile a brief summary of the discussion on each agenda item and later circulate mimeographed or printed copies to all those who were present. Many groups make use of interim committees to investigate and report back on problems requiring research and analysis, and one or two have permanent research arms, as does the Association of Australian State Road Authorities with its recently established Australian Road Research Board.

Basically, all the conferences have two major goals: to provide their members with information about the practices and procedures of the other states in their particular field of interest, and to assist the states in achieving some degree of uniformity between them. The aims of the Association of Government Printers of Australasia are typical of those of most of the conferences. For "printing," read any of the other functions with which the states are concerned. Its aims are declared to be: "(a) To diffuse information among members and to promote uniformity of style and format in public printing and stationery. (b) To encourage greater efficiency in the purchase and production of public printing and stationery. (c) To effect improvements in methods of distribution and control. (d) To facilitate the exchange of information on new printing processes, production methods and equipment. (e) To keep association members up to date with any modern improvement in method of production adopted by any member. (f) To provide a regular exchange between members of publications, brochures and other examples of Government Printing."[2]

All of the groups serve a secondary purpose, not often enunciated but which is nonetheless felt—to preserve the field for state action against Commonwealth encroachment. The states reason that in unity there is strength and that a demonstration of unanimity is their best protection. Since the differences between the many conferences are more in the topics discussed and in the issues presented than in the practices and procedures they employ, only a few of them need to be described at any length to give a general understanding of them all.

Conference of State Public Service Commissioners

One of the most important conferences is that of the state public service commissioners. Since government is the major employer in Australia, the standards and procedures of state personnel systems are of immediate concern to Australia's growth and development, and by and large, for the last twenty-five years, at least, those standards and procedures

[2] Mimeographed statement supplied by the Government Printer of New South Wales.

have been worked out through the Conference of Public Service Commissioners. The conference actually consists of the commissioner from each state and his assistants, though the chairman of the Commonwealth Public Service Board, the commissioner for Papua and New Guinea, and the equivalent officers in New Zealand are regularly invited to sit in. It first began to meet in 1937 and now meets every two years. There is no secretariat. The commissioner of the host state presides and his office services the meeting, including preparing the agenda and taking and circulating the minutes. The conference rarely if ever comes to the point of taking formal action, and as a matter of policy it does not publish official reports of its meetings. It often makes submissions and recommendations to the Premiers' Conference. Discussions range widely over the field of public service, but questions concerning salaries are most important to the commissioners. The agenda for the 1960 meeting in Brisbane featured among others the following topics: employment of married women, preference in employment to ex-servicemen, employment of the physically handicapped, equal pay for men and women, the use of electronic data processing, Colombo Plan trainees, employment of aliens, appeals systems, and disability allowances. Some of the items on the agenda are raised merely to inform; others are discussed with a view toward finding ways of collaboration and of achieving uniformity. At the 1960 meeting, for example, the question of the exchange of officers between the states was brought up for discussion. Very little of this has ever been done, and the conference explored the possibilities of expanding the practice.[3] Other meetings have discussed the adoption of uniform practices among the states with regard to superannuation, long service leaves, and certain salary scales.

At first, the conference produced a manual of information

[3] The 1960 meeting was reported in detail in Queensland Government Public Relations Bureau, *News Bulletin*, November 22, 1960, p. 2.

about personnel practices in the several states, but keeping it up to date was difficult, and the project was reluctantly abandoned. Had it been continued, it probably would have produced some degree of uniformity singlehandedly, as the states learned from it how problems were being solved and functions performed in other states and adopted those ways themselves. But the meetings of the conference provide a great deal of opportunity for exchange in any case, and considerable contact takes place between meetings as well. Through the years a spirit of friendliness and cooperation has been built up among the commissioners, with the result that fairly uniform policies on salaries, leaves, discipline, and training have been formulated by the states, and the end product has been the general improvement of Australian administrative standards.[4]

Australian Port Authorities Association

Also of key importance to Australia's economy are the management and development of its ports, for the nation is heavily dependent upon overseas trade. But port administration lies chiefly within the province of the states[5] and in fact each port is operated largely on an individual basis. Through an interstate device, however—the Australian Port Authorities Association—the managers of all the Australian ports are brought together regularly, and a large degree of uniformity in practice among the ports is achieved in the process. The

[4] See memorandum, "Interstate Relations of State Departments and Bodies: Public Service Board," Public Service Board of New South Wales, copy supplied to author by the Under Secretary of the Premier's Department. G. A. Gray to author, July 14, 1960.

[5] Australian ports come primarily within one of the following classifications. They are administered: (1) by the Commonwealth government (the port of Darwin through the Northern Territory Administration); (2) by the state government (the ports of Queensland through the Department of Harbours and Marine); (3) by a statutory authority (the South Australia Harbours Board and the Maritime Services Board of New South Wales for the harbors of those states); (4) by local boards or trusts (Tasmania, Victoria, and Western Australia have established a local board for each port).

association dates from 1948, although Interstate Harbour Conferences began to be held as early as 1916. Thirty-three port authorities now belong to the Association, which is quite a formal body with a detailed constitution,[6] an elaborate system of sharing the costs of the association's activities, and a permanent head office and secretariat supplied by the Melbourne Harbour Trust. The full association meets biennially, but a permanent committee, chosen by the members, meets three or four times a year and manages the bulk of the association's business. Each member authority usually sends several representatives to the meetings, so that there are about sixty delegates. A number of observers from New Zealand and from English port authorities are normally invited to attend as well. The meetings last several days—the 1958 session at Cairns ran into the fifth day. At the conclusion of each meeting, the association passes a series of resolutions, which, along with a summary of the discussion during the meeting, are printed and subsequently distributed to all those in attendance.

The association is principally concerned with the exchange of knowledge about handling port problems and with securing uniformity in port practices. Indeed, its constitution specifically enjoins the association to secure uniformity. Subjects on the agenda of recent meetings include the development of a uniform approach to charging wharfage on exports, the possibilities of a uniform buoyage system, and the issuance of uniform third-class marine engine driver's certificates. The sixteenth conference, in 1958, considered fifty-six subjects altogether, and in almost every case the resolution adopted by the association urged cooperation on its members. In addition to discussing such problems and arriving at acceptable joint solutions at its meetings, the association also works to draft standard codes for adoption by all the port authorities

[6] The constitution of the association, which is currently undergoing revision, is treated as confidential by the association's leadership.

in Australia. Codes have been developed for the safe handling of dangerous goods—explosives and flammable liquids—and handling refinery goods in port, for preventing and fighting fires on ships at berth, and, most recently, for regulating nuclear-powered ships in port. Every year, the codes are adopted by a number of additional authorities. It is safe to predict that before long there will be a single approach to all these matters throughout the country.

Following a decision of the eleventh conference, in 1948, that it would be advantageous to discuss harbor engineering problems separately, a subordinate Conference of Harbour Engineers was created in 1952. The members of the association are circularized by the permanent committee as to the subjects to be discussed by the conference, which follows the pattern of its parent body at its meetings. The conference is more a reporting body than anything else, however. Its meetings feature the reading of papers on such subjects as breakwater and wharf construction, fendering, tidal and wave protection, and dredging. They also give association members additional opportunities to inspect other harbor installations.

The association has been particularly productive of interstate cooperation.[7] As a result of its work, port administration, which might otherwise vary from port to port, has already been coordinated to a considerable extent, and the years ahead will no doubt see the adoption of still more common standards.

National Association of Australian State Road Authorities

Another established body is the National Association of Australian State Road Authorities,[8] which represents the central road construction authorities in the states. It was estab-

---

[7] *Sixteenth Conference of the Australian Port Authorities Association, . . . 1958, Report Containing Summary of Resolutions, Minutes . . . and . . . Debates* (Brisbane, 1958), p. 43.

[8] See *supra*, p. 64.

lished as a conference in 1934 and has served ever since to provide a means "of pooling technical and administrative experience; of inaugurating, co-ordinating and rationalising road research projects; of harmonising and co-ordinating standards; of ascertaining and publishing the facts about Australia's principal roads and their financing; and of developing an informed outlook on Australia's road problems."[9] The annual meeting of the association is attended by the administrative heads of the seven road building bodies in Australia; the road constructing authority of the Commonwealth is a member by reason of the Commonwealth's responsibility for roads in the territories. Technical work is handled by a Principal Technical Committee, which in turn is assisted by a number of specialist subcommittees. The technical committees meet as often as necessary throughout the year. Secretarial services are provided by one of the member authorities, with each member contributing toward the expenses. The association is unique among its sister conferences in that it has employed a full-time executive engineer to serve in a coordinating and administrative capacity and to pay particular attention to the design and operational aspects of roads. In the course of its work, the association addresses itself to all the major problems encountered in road construction and operation: traffic, road-making materials, planning, mechanical equipment, vehicle limits and standards, bridge and road design, road statistics, mapping, and naming highways. It has been especially active in securing uniformity among the states in numbering highways and in bringing about uniform pavement markings. Recently it has been attempting to provide some uniformity in the priorities assigned to road construction by the several governments. At the 1960 meeting in Hobart, the present road situation in Australia was discussed at length, and it was

[9] National Association of Australian State Road Authorities, *Australian Roads* (1956), p. 33.

agreed that the immediate objective of the association's members should be the construction of an interregional road system in continental Australia, with routes connecting all the capital cities and principal regions of population with one another.

Roads in Australia are built by the states with federal aid, but the Commonwealth government does not impose limitations on the use of the funds to achieve uniformity, as the federal government does in the United States. Instead, the association works for uniformity, not only by developing a pattern of national highways for adoption by the states, but also by assuring a uniform degree of quality in terms of highway design and construction. Under the association's auspices, standard specifications for bridge construction and road design have been developed and accepted by all the road-building authorities in the Commonwealth. The only force the association exerts on its members to coordinate their activities is pressure to accept the logic of a single system of roads for all Australia. In 1961 it undertook to make a survey of road needs for the next ten years, and its findings can be expected to receive a good deal of publicity both at the association's meetings and through publications, thus adding to the pressure for uniformity in construction.

Interviews with state officials all over Australia made it clear to me that the association's own evaluation of its role is generally accepted as being correct: "Year by year as the Association has continued it has found that co-operation between the States has steadily grown and an increasingly broad viewpoint has emerged. The road problems of one State become, to some degree, the concern of all States, and gradually a national outlook develops, free from inhibitions based on State boundaries. The habit of co-operation based on personal contacts provides a firm support to the work of the Association."[10]

[10] *Ibid.*

Conference of Australasian Prison Administrators

Unlike the representatives of the port authorities and road construction groups, which have been meeting together for a long time and whose organization has become quite formal, the state prison administrators have only been meeting for a few years and so far have done so very informally.[11] Their first annual meeting was in 1959. Their conferences have purposely been run as forums, with each member free to accept or reject what was propounded on the floor. Discussion has not resulted in the adoption of resolutions.[12] In a number of cases, however, the delegates agreed to make representations to the political heads of their departments with a view to action at that level. One important matter so dealt with was the arrangement for the supervision of parolees of one state who are resident during parole in another state. Another was the mechanism for interstate cooperation in research. Other items that have been under discussion include the possibility of establishing a joint training institute for senior officers in the Australasian and Pacific prison services, the standardization of the terminology used to classify prison staff, and the desirability of exchanging staff between prison units. A number of programs for cooperation in prisoner care have also been suggested. Because the prison administrators have been late in organizing their conference, they can benefit from the experiences of the older groups and can adopt many of their practices and procedures. Prison officers are enthusiastic about the possibilities their conference has opened up and expect to develop a large number of interstate relationships as rapidly as they can.

[11] The Conference of Australasian Prison Administrators includes, in addition to the head penal officer in each state, the prison administrators in the Northern Territory, Papua–New Guinea, and New Zealand, as well as representatives of universities that have departments of criminology, as observers.
[12] J. S. Morony, Comptroller General of Prisons, New South Wales, to author, November 9, 1962.

Summary of Other Groups

It is tempting to go on describing in capsule form a number of other groups of state officials. For the most part their activities have been ignored, and it is time someone looked at all these groups as case studies in public administration, if not also as devices designed to facilitate the operation of Australian federalism. They are important in both respects, and our knowledge of Australian government is so much the poorer for lack of such studies. The Conference of State Police Commissioners and its subunits, for example, have been instrumental in bringing about far closer cooperation among state police departments in Australia than exists among local police units in the United States; in the process the efficiency of each individual department has been increased. At least, this seems to be the case. But so long as the story of police cooperation remains untold, the lessons it contains for effective federalism remains obscure as well. Similarly, it appears that the Australian and New Zealand Railways Conference goes far toward unifying Australia's otherwise divided railway system. This conference, however, has not been subjected to analysis either, and its importance is thus less generally recognized than it probably ought to be. There is every indication that the handling of Australian forestry matters has been improved as a result of the work of the Conference of State Foresters, and that the Biennial Interstate Fauna Conference is responsible for a great deal of coordination of state activities in the field of fauna conservation. These assertions, too, ought to be tested. Indeed, all these groups, and the others listed at the beginning of this chapter, ought to be studied for the lessons they have to teach not only to students of Australian federalism in particular but also to those of federalism generally. If the data were available, it would probably show that each group makes a sizable contribution to interstate cooperation and so to the successful functioning of the Australian federal system. As the study of Australian government is expanded in the next few years, as it is very likely to be, the activities of these conferences ought to be given priority in research.

Nongovernmental Organizations

Interstate cooperation is not solely the product of conferences of state officials themselves. State officials also attend the myriad meetings of national and regional professional, technical, and trade associations, labor unions, and employer organizations that are as common in Australia as they are in the United States, and here they lay groundwork for the subsequent development of cooperative arrangements. No one keeps a list of such organizations, but virtually every field of state governmental activity is paralleled by some kind of organization that gives its members occasion to consult and collaborate. At every meeting, one or more administrators from the state departments concerned are likely to be found. State health department officials, for example, attend the meetings of the Royal Australasian College of Physicians, the Royal Institute of Health, and other hospital and medical associations. In recent years, representatives of the Department of Public Health in New South Wales have attended conferences sponsored by the British Psychological Society, the Australian College of Speech Therapists, the Australian Association of Psychiatrists, the Australian Medical Congress, the Australian Society of Neurologists, and the Institute of Food Technology.[13] State education officers attend the meetings of such groups as the Australian Teachers' Federation, the Australian College of Education, and the Australian Council for Educational Research. State forestry officials attend meetings of pulp and paper trade associations, state labor department representatives, meetings of labor unions

13 G. A. Gray to author.

and employers' groups, state tourist officers, meetings of the Australian National Travel Association, and state agricultural officers, meetings of such organizations as the Australian Dried Fruits Association. Meetings of the Australian Association for the Advancement of Science, the Royal Australian Chemical Institute, and the Institution of Engineers, Australia, give technical people from a variety of state agencies still other chances to meet and discuss their problems. A number of state departments even reported to me that UNESCO meetings of one sort or another had proved helpful in bringing state officials together and especially in getting them to agree on the collection and dissemination of uniform statistics in several areas of action.[14] Finally, some additional opportunity for contact is provided by meetings of international organizations, to which Australians, public and lay alike, belong in great numbers. State electricity commission members, for instance, attend meetings of the World Power Conference,[15] and other state officers go to meetings of similar international bodies in their own fields of activity.

Standards Association of Australia

One organization in particular deserves special mention because it directs its programs in part at bringing about coordination among the states in a number of state functions. That is the Standards Association of Australia. The Standards Association's charter from the Commonwealth government includes the following objectives directly involving interstate

[14] The Commonwealth Government ordinarily arranges and finances the delegates' travel to UNESCO meetings. To the extent that it does so, this is another contribution that the Commonwealth makes to the development of interstate cooperation.

[15] The Sixth Plenary Session of the World Power Conference was held in Melbourne, October 20–27, 1962. Virtually every state official who is concerned with the supply and use of energy from various sources, including coal, oil, gas, and electricity, attended the sessions. The chairman of the state electricity commission of Victoria served as conference chairman. *Australia in Facts and Figures*, No. 76 (December quarter 1962), p. 79.

cooperation: "(a) To prepare and promote the general adoption of standards relating to structures, commodities, materials, practices, operations, matters and things and from time to time revise, alter and amend the same. . . . (c) To co-ordinate the efforts of producers and users for the improvement of materials, products, appliances, processes and methods. . . . (g) To collect and circulate statistics and other information relative to standardisation in all its branches (h) To provide for the delivery and holding of lectures, exhibitions, public meetings, classes and conferences calculated to advance directly or indirectly the cause of . . . standardisation, whether general or technical. . . . (j) To communicate information to members on all matters affecting the practice of standardisation. . . . (l) To promote or support changes in the law designed or likely to help all or any of the objects of the Association."[16] Each of the states is officially represented on the council of the association, and the association is financed in part by annual contributions from the state governments. The association works principally through individual subject-matter committees, made up of representatives both of industry and of the states, rather than through general meetings. The committees, composed of technical experts, develop sets of standards to recommend for adoption by the states. To use state electricity commissions as examples again, members of each commission, along with representatives of a wide range of electrical interests in Australia, are members of the association's Wiring Rules Sectional Committee. That committee drafts wiring rules, which then become the standard for electrical installation work throughout the country. The commissions are also members of the Electrical Approvals Standards Committee, which prepares approvals and test specifications covering materials, fittings, accessories, appli-

16 "Extract from Royal Charter and Bye-Laws of Standards Association of Australia," mimeographed release supplied me by the central office of the association. See also B. B. Bryant, "The Standards Association of Australia," *Public Administration*, V (September 1945), 303–18.

ances, and apparatus used in electrical installations. The committee also prescribes standards of construction with which manufacturers must comply before electrical appliances and equipment are sold for connection to the supply mains of state electricity commissions. The association of course has no power to enforce its rules as standards, but they are so carefully drawn up that the states accept them readily. Indeed, mutual acceptance of the association's standards greatly simplifies the work of technical units of the Australian state governments and saves the states both time and money as well. All the state railway systems in Australia, the Departments of Mines, and the several state road authorities make use of these standards, and all attest to the benefits they derive from doing so. Through the services it performs, the Standards Association brings a large degree of uniform practice among the states and so makes a distinctive contribution to interstate cooperation.

Ad Hoc State Conferences

Finally, as the Commonwealth does occasionally in the fields of its interest, the states also often call ad hoc conferences when special problems of universal concern arise. A Conference of Rural Fire Authorities, for example, was held in Sydney in 1955, where the matter of interstate cooperation in bush fire fighting was discussed, and a Conference on Fire Weather Forecasting brought all the state forestry departments together in Melbourne in 1959.

Too much should probably not be claimed for conferences as contributors to interstate cooperation, despite their obvious importance. Since no conference has the power to bind the participating states, in the last analysis each state acts independently. When all the states take the same or similar actions in the wake of a meeting, as happens very often,

uniformity or coordination results, and the conference receives
the credit. When different actions—or no action at all—follow
a meeting, and this is sometimes the case, the conference can
do little about it, at least in the short run. Nor do all conferences contribute equally to interstate cooperation. Some
subject-matter areas lend themselves to collaboration better
than others, and for purely personal or party reasons, the
persons at one meeting may get along better with each other
than those at another. For these reasons alone, conferences
are bound to vary considerably in productive results. In a
number of cases, the various state representatives are not really
on an equal basis at a conference meeting. New South Wales
and Victoria are the dominant states, and their proposals are
sometimes resisted by the less important states for that reason
alone. And the governmental machinery in the states differs,
with the result that states cannot always carry out conference
recommendations in the same way. The recommendations
of the Public Service Commissioners' Conference, for instance, will be carried out differently in Western Australia,
where the Public Service Commissioner is primarily a classify-
ing authority, than in New South Wales and Victoria, where
the public service boards do both classification and salary
determination. The same kind of variations affect coordination in many other fields of action.

Moreover, conference meetings that take place only biennially, or even at intervals of eighteen months or a year,
cannot be expected to bring about full interstate understanding and cooperation by themselves. For one thing, there is
enough turnover in personnel that rapport cannot be assumed
to exist each time a conference convenes. For another, conference agenda are usually so full that, in spite of good intentions, meetings tend to become more reporting sessions than
occasions for discussion and evolution of uniform policies.
And in most cases, it is only the department or agency head
who attends the conferences regularly, or at the most, the

head officer and an immediate subordinate or two. Unless they do an effective job of communication—and inspiration—on their return home, the goal of cooperation, however well articulated at the meeting, does not get down through the rank and file of the agency or department concerned. Finally, except for the Premiers' Conferences, the conferences deal only with particular problems. None are concerned with the general problems of the states in Australia. A great many individual state trees are thus nourished by interstate action, so to speak, but no one attends to the forest as a whole.

The meetings of the almost two-score state organizations is not the sole reason for their importance. Since the size of the meetings is comparatively small, the representatives have the opportunity to become well acquainted and consequently after their meetings will carry on a great deal more informal consultation, planning, and action among themselves than they might otherwise have done. Some cooperation, of course, has always taken place among state officers simply as a matter of courtesy in answering queries and requests for help. Virtually every state officer whom I interviewed assured me, however, that such exchanges were at a bare minimum until the postwar growth of interstate conferences was well under way with resulting personal contacts and friendships. By 1960 there was almost unanimous agreement that state officials helped one another far beyond the demands of ordinary courtesy. As one state official commented, in the field of "personal relations and contacts . . . there [is] ready co-operation . . . [;] in the main a very satisfactory level of give and take exists."[17]

This interim "give and take" takes many forms: the exchange of annual reports and periodic publications with counterpart officers in other states; consultation as specific problems arise in person or by telephone with officials in other

[17] G. G. Pearson, Minister of Works and Minister of Marine, State of South Australia, to author, January 13, 1960.

states; replying to requests for information by mail; personal visits of inspection or to make use of another state's facilities; the regular exchange of laws, regulations, standards, and codes as they are developed; and advice from other states in the course of drawing up new legislation. As a byproduct of the Conference of State Housing Ministers and Officers, for example, close liaison is constantly maintained between the several state housing authorities, who exchange information on subjects of mutual interest from time to time. "Typical of this type of interchange," reports the Minister of Housing of New South Wales, "is a recent communication from the Department of Housing, Tasmania, seeking information as to whether the Commission provides multi-outlet television antennae in its multi-unit flat buildings and if so, [whether] any special charges [are] levied upon those using the service and how such charges [are] calculated and collected."[18] Another typical inquiry was a request from Victoria for details of a scheme of home sale with a minimum deposit. In both cases, and in many another like them, the information sought was freely supplied. Each state housing authority prepares an annual report. Copies of these reports are exchanged between the states as are copies of any other bulletins or pamphlets that may be issued from time to time. In addition, state authorities are occasionally visited by representatives from housing authorities in other states. Usually, every courtesy is extended to the visitors, and arrangements are made for them to visit local offices and to inspect housing estates and government flat projects if they wish to do so. The housing example could be multiplied many times. There is not a field of state government activity that boasts a conference that is not also marked by a vast amount of informal contact across state lines between meetings.

Departments and agencies that have not yet developed a

[18] Minister of Housing to the Under Secretary, Premier's Department, July 29, 1960, copy supplied to author.

conference of their own also exchange information and assistance. The Secretary of the Parliamentary Public Works Committee of Victoria reported that he has often had occasion to seek information from other states and that without exception "each State of the Commonwealth has expressed its willingness to co-operate with the Committee in every way possible to obtain information which would assist it in its deliberations on matters under review . . . . Conferences have been arranged with appropriate Ministers and with top level representatives of Departments and Authorities and with other persons concerned with a particular project and comprehensive inspections have been arranged and the expenses thereof met so as to ensure that the Committee would be able to obtain the fullest possible information. As a result of visits to other States, the Committee has been able to see what has been and is being done there regarding similar projects to those under consideration in Victoria [and] has been greatly assisted in reaching final conclusions and making recommendations."[19] In the same way, the departments of local government in the states regularly exchange copies of legislation with their counterparts in other states and respond to pleas for information on particular questions as they arise. "For example, a proposal was recently put forward in [Victoria] for a municipal insurance pool to be conducted by the State Accident Insurance Office for the benefit of Victorian municipalities. The Western Australian Government has established a . . . pool on these lines and information on the functioning of this pool was obtained to assist in assessing the Victorian proposal. Similarly information has been sought recently by other States as to the conditions under which coin operated petrol pumps are permitted in this State."[20]

Thus through their own conferences, as well as through

[19] J. D. O'Carroll, Secretary, Parliamentary Public Works Committee, to the Secretary, Premier's Department, May 5, 1960, copy supplied to author.
[20] P. P. Mithen, Secretary for Local Government, Victoria, to the Secretary, Premier's Department, March 22, 1960, copy supplied to author.

those convened by the Commonwealth, and through the interim personal contacts that are the natural byproducts of both, the Australian states have moved closer together in recent years in many of the fields of state government activity. This movement has been casual and usually informal, and states have not always moved at the same rate, but the trend has been steady, and the working both of the Australian federal system generally and of the state governments particularly is stronger as a result. Additional conferences will probably be organized in the years just ahead, and as they are, the benefits of interstate cooperation that they engender will be extended into still other areas of state administration.

Chapter 5 THE STATES AND
INTERSTATE COOPERATION:
FORMAL ARRANGEMENTS

Although most methods of interstate cooperation in Australia
are informal, not all of them are. A variety of formal arrangements have been developed as well, distinguished from the
informal ones chiefly by their end product, which in every
case involves the use of one state's facilities or services by
another, the passage of complementary legislation, the recognition of the acts or papers of one state as valid in others, or the
joint conduct of a specific interstate activity. Through such
arrangements, officers of one state perform functions for
officers of another or exchange places with one another, the
services or facilities of one state are made available for use by
officials or citizens of another, or two or more states join with
each other, and sometimes with the Commonwealth, in
carrying on an enterprise or activity. In some cases the
practice is rooted in custom alone; in others, statutory
authority has been necessary. In every case, these arrangements serve to prevent undue duplication of effort and thus
to effect economy in state operations.

In most of the formal arrangments that have been developed, the natural sequence has been from informal contact
to formal cooperation. As state officers come to know each
other and each other's problems through conferences and
other informal devices, collaboration and assistance across
state lines take place almost automatically. In Australia,
where mateship may have the same hold on state officials it
has on the public at large,[1] the pressure for a helping hand is

especially strong. Indeed, there is probably no limit to inter-state arrangements of this kind save the needs and imagination of the officers involved. Friendship alone cannot be counted on to produce complementary legislation, reciprocal action, or joint interstate activities, however. Complementary legislation demands virtual agreement on details as well as on principles, and thus is more difficult than merely extending a helping hand. Reciprocity too can exist only where there are no basic divergences or policy disagreements among the states and thus is confined to relatively unimportant matters. As for joint enterprises, both the geographic relation of the states, one to the others, and the distribution of population within them work against the development of interstate administration on the same scale as has occurred in the United States.[2] Only four of the six Australian states are located so as to make feasible joint enterprises involving physical facilities. Although there are some possibilities for the future, the number of joint enterprises will remain understandably small.

The Performance of Services for Another State

Examples of arrangements under which officials of one state perform services for officers of another state are common. They range from the simple performance of clerical or recording functions to much more extensive and involved services. One or two illustrations will be enough to show what kinds of things are done. One of the most important services performed interstate is in connection with practice before the

[1] R. F. Brissenden in "The Australian Image," *Hemisphere*, VI (January 1962), 8, cautions that mateship, "the central element in the Australian tradition should not . . . be simply accepted as a fact. . . .[Its] role as a moral force in contemporary Australian life should be thoroughly re-investigated. . . . [The] central place of mateship certainly cannot be taken for granted."

[2] See Leach and Sugg, *Administration of Interstate Compacts*, and Richard H. Leach, "Interstate Authorities in the United States," *Law and Contemporary Problems*, XXVI (Autumn 1961), 666–81.

High Court. The High Court of Australia is a court of appeals from the supreme courts of the states. It sits in the various state capitals in turn. To facilitate the transaction of the states' legal work, there is a long-standing arrangement under which the crown solicitor of each state acts as agent for the crown solicitor of each of the other states in handling legal matters arising in that state. This service is chiefly made available in connection with proceedings before the High Court, but it is not limited to that. It covers all types of legal work that one state might have to have performed in another. The Crown Solicitor of New South Wales, for example, has acted in conveyancing matters for Queensland on a number of occasions and has frequently been called on to assist in extradition cases. In any twelve-month period, each of the crown solicitors will find themselves performing services like these for any or all of their sister states, and they will do it without any strict accounting of what they have done. The legal work of all the states is thus greatly facilitated. In the same way, the several public trustees (public curators, in some states) act for one another when it is necessary to collect the assets of a deceased person held in another state. Quite regularly insurance claims are settled by one state government insurance office on behalf of another state office where the insured is temporarily a resident of the other state. The departments of public works and of mines in the several states have developed arrangements for inspecting equipment being manufactured for a sister department out of state. And by arrangement between the states, the responsibility for inter-state migrants is accepted by the state immigration authority under whose jurisdiction they happen to be. In any of these cases no more is needed to secure action than a telephone call or a letter between the officials concerned. Other examples might be cited—they seem to be legion—but they would only show that departments and agencies in every aspect of state government perform services for officers of other states as a regular part of their own jobs. The burden is not very onerous on any of the states, and the state department heads I interviewed did not even bother to keep records of the interstate services their units carried on. All state officials, however, are conscious of the help they receive in this way and are quick to say how much it means to the better administration of their particular department or agency.

In a number of cases arrangements have been worked out for the exchange of personnel between state agencies. Usually only a few persons are involved at a time, and there are normally special reasons for the exchange. Most often, it is to permit the officer or officers concerned to acquire a special kind of experience that he needs in his home post and could not get any other way. Teacher exchanges have also been made occasionally. The personnel involved in an exchange continue to be paid by their home departments and usually remain away no longer than a year. In at least one instance, however, officers from one state have been permanently assigned to a department in another. The two states in which the main flow of interstate road traffic occurs in Australia— Victoria and New South Wales—have each found it expedient to station a full-time staff member in the office of the other's road transport authority to answer inquiries accurately and assist in solving problems involving interstate transport. This pattern could of course be utilized in other fields.

The Use of Services or Facilities of Other States

The extension by one state of the privilege of using its facilities or taking advantage of its services has likewise become quite common. Again, these arrangements vary from the simple to the complex. Thus loans of works of art owned by one state are frequently made to the art galleries of other states, and loans of anthropological, geological, and zoological material are made between state museums. An elaborate interstate interlibrary-loan system has been developed for both books and films. On occasion, drilling equipment is loaned or exchanged between state mines departments. Public electricity supply is a function of the Australian states, and arrangements have been made both between New South Wales and Queensland and between New South Wales and Victoria under which electricity can be supplied across state borders with a minimum of formalities. At the other end of the scale are the arrangements made under an agreement between the premiers of New South Wales and South Australia and the Broken Hill Water Board, later ratified by legislation passed by the respective parliaments in 1953 and 1954, to supply water to the uranium field at Radium Hill, South Australia, from the Umberumberka reservoir in New South Wales. South Australia was authorized to construct and maintain whatever works were needed in New South Wales and to hold the land on which the works were built. Somewhat similar arrangements have been made, this time by agreement between town councils, for the town of Tweed Heads in New South Wales to draw its water from the adjoining town of Coolangatta in Queensland. Consideration is now being given to the possibility that the two towns might work out a comparable arrangement for the discharge and treatment of sewage. School services are also extended across state lines. For example, as a result of agreements reached between the Education Departments of Victoria, Queensland, and New South Wales, children residing in certain border districts are permitted to cross the border to attend school in another state. They may even compete for scholarships and bursaries, provided they have been in attendance at the out-of-state school for twelve months prior to the award. Tasmania makes use of the Victoria Department of Health's leprosy hospital for the treatment of its victims of that disease.[3] At the request of the state of South Australia,

[3] The details of the Tasmanian examples were supplied to me in an interview with Mr. Kenneth Binns, Under Treasurer of Tasmania, Hobart, Tasmania, October 20, 1961.

the Co-ordinating Board of Queensland[4] carried out aerial poisoning campaigns against dingoes in South Australia.

Perhaps the most extensive sharing of facilities which has been worked out among the states is the pooling of state railway systems for interstate traffic. Although the systems in Australia are absolutely independent of one another—as is evidenced by the fact that they have not yet been able to achieve complete uniformity of gage—they have nevertheless developed a quite satisfactory arrangement for sharing their track and equipment with one another. By agreement embodied in legislation between the governments of Victoria and South Australia, and between those of Victoria and New South Wales, certain mileages of 5′ 3″ railway are operated by the Victorian Railways in those two states.[5] In addition, each system works in close cooperation with the other systems in the handling of through interstate traffic. The various systems, again by formal agreement, fix freight rates and fares and conditions for the interstate transport of goods and passengers. Through-booking of passengers, parcels, and freight can be arranged between any two stations in Australia as a result. Each system makes a monthly financial settlement with all the other systems, in which the revenue due each from the carriage of interstate traffic is allocated. The settlement also covers the adjustment of claims which are met as agreed on between the systems. Because the greater part of the railway system of South Australia is of the same gage as that of Victoria (5′3″), a more intimate relationship exists between the Victorian and South Australian railways than

[4] A board provided for in the Stock Routes and Rural Lands Protection Acts, 1944–1951, to carry out programs for the control and destruction of animal pests and noxious plants.

[5] In the case of South Australia, the mileage consists of two short sections linking with the South Australian 5′ 3″ lines at Mt. Gambier and Innaroo, respectively. In New South Wales, three lines are operated—to Oaklands, Deniliquin, and Balranald; only the first of these connects with New South Wales standard-gage lines. The total length of the lines operated by the Victorian Railways in New South Wales is two hundred miles.

between any of the others. This relationship includes the through-working of rolling stock (except locomotives) and to a limited extent of staff (on the through expresses between Melbourne and Adelaide). The rolling stock that makes up the overnight expresses between the two capital cities is jointly owned, the cost being shared on the basis of route mileage. Freight rolling stock is individually owned, and each system pays an interchange charge when its stock is on the lines of any of the other systems. For many years, all the railways of New South Wales were constructed on the standard gage, and there was therefore no physical interworking between the Victorian railways and those of New South Wales. The same close cooperation as exists between Victoria and South Australia, however, was maintained in the handling of interstate traffic. Just recently, a new standard gage line was opened from the border town of Albury, in New South Wales, to Melbourne, enabling through passenger service to operate for the first time between Melbourne and Sydney, and freight trains to operate between Melbourne and any point on the New South Wales system. It is possible now, too, to travel via standard gage from Sydney to Brisbane. These developments have led to the same kind of working arrangements between those states that have long existed between Victoria and South Australia.

Once again, a great many other instances in which facilities are shared by one state with another could be described. The ones I have discussed are only a small part of those reported to me by state officials, but no more need be cited here to make the point about their range and the wide extent of their use. For the most part, the state officers who gave examples were not inclined to make anything much of them, taking them more or less for granted. Better than anything else, this attitude on their part reveals the degree to which this type of interstate cooperation has been integrated into the operation of Australian state government.

Complementary Legislation

Complementary legislation is not very common in Australia. The most important examples relate to the marketing of agricultural products and are the result of the work of the Australian Agricultural Council, which is responsible for the fact that there is more cooperation in primary industry and in agriculture than in any other areas of state activity in Australia. The Australian Wheat Board was set up in 1946 by all the states and the Commonwealth, in association with Commonwealth legislation for the stabilization of the price of wheat. Its functions are to receive, handle, and market all wheat produced in Australia and to pay the growers for their crops. In years of favorable prices, it makes contributions to the Stabilizing Committee, which manages the fund used to subsidize the price of wheat in unfavorable years. The Australian Dried Fruits Board was established in 1934 on somewhat similar lines but does not act in conjunction with legislation for a stabilization program. The Australian Barley Board was created in 1947 by South Australia and Victoria. Unlike the other programs, it does not involve the Commonwealth. The Barley Board buys and sells the barley, oats, and sorghum produced in the two states. All three boards have enjoyed success with their constituents, and their lives have been extended a number of times.

The sale of table margarine has been controlled by complementary legislation, but the Australian Agricultural Council at its fifty-seventh meeting (July 1962) resolved that, inasmuch as problems "have arisen in administering the existing legislation because of weaknesses concerning production quotas," uniform legislation, rather than complementary legislation, had become desirable.[6]

The problem of pollution of coastal areas by oil was also

6 *Australia in Facts and Figures*, No. 75, p. 75.

handled by complementary legislation. The passage of complementary acts by both the Commonwealth and the states permitted Australia to ratify the International Convention on the Prevention of Pollution of the Sea by Oil.

Finally, the whole approach to controlling monopolies and restrictive trade practices is currently under study in Australia, and the possibility that they might be controlled by complementary legislation has been raised in the House of Representatives.[7] Whether the Commonwealth government will decide to act on the suggestion remains to be seen.

Reciprocity

Reciprocity exists in a number of areas of state government activity in Australia. By and large, it results from administrative rather than legislative action and extends to relatively minor areas of concern. Since the turn of the century, for example, there has been complete reciprocity between the Surveyors Boards in all the states. As a result, a surveyor registered in any Australian state may register in any other state merely by complying with minimal requirements rather than by having to take another qualifying examination. For many years there have been reciprocal agreements among the states on motor vehicle registrations and drivers' licenses. Reciprocity also exists among the state railway systems to cover interstate rail travel for railway employees on annual leave and railway officials on departmental business.

Joint Enterprises

If less common, joint interstate activities are more dramatic types of formal interstate cooperation than any of those so far described. As a result, they are almost always mentioned first by Australians themselves and are given the most pub-

[7] *Ibid.*, No. 76, pp. 34–37.

licity. This probably has the effect of overemphasizing their importance in the picture of interstate cooperation. Over the years more attention has probably been paid to the River Murray Commission than to all the other examples of interstate cooperation in Australia. As a matter of fact, interstate joint enterprises are relatively few in number and account for only a fraction of the total amount of interstate cooperation. Like the other types of formal cooperation, there is no single pattern that they follow. Some are only temporary in nature and involve nothing physical. In 1961, to cite an instance, several of the states joined together to argue a case before the Privy Council, *Dennis Hotels Pty. Ltd. v. Victoria.*[8] The case involved the propriety of the state of Victoria's levying a license fee on victuallers—in short, a liquor tax. The action was challenged by Dennis Hotel, a Victorian pub, on the ground that such a tax was an excise and therefore not within the province of the state government. Tasmania, Western Australia, and South Australia all had similar licensing acts, and thus all saw their own revenue structures in jeopardy if the tax were invalidated. When the decision went against Victoria at home and an appeal was made to the Privy Council, therefore, all the states involved agreed to pool their resources and to employ a single attorney to represent them all before the Privy Council. The Solicitor General of Tasmania, D. M. Chambers, took on the job, with the understanding that the costs incurred were to be apportioned among the states on the basis of population. As it turned out, the case was decided on a technicality, and its merits were never argued.

The states have also joined with each other and with the Commonwealth government in a Standing Committee on Overseas Investment. The purpose of the committee is to discuss methods whereby the promotion of private overseas

[8] Privy Council No. 7 of 1961; see the *Weekly Law Reports*, III (July 14, 1961), 202-81, for a full presentation of the case.

investment in Australia may be coordinated and streamlined while preserving the independence of the states in making approaches to potential investors. The committee has only begun to function, but all the states have shown their willingness to cooperate in the enterprise and are hopeful of beneficial results.

Other joint activities are permanently established. The state public libraries, for example, cooperate in maintaining a union list of periodicals, newspapers, and monographs through the Australian Advisory Council on Bibliographical Services, on which each of the libraries is represented. The Victoria Free Library Service Board and the Library Board of New South Wales provide joint library service through three interstate regional library schemes to a number of towns along the upper Murray River. And New South Wales and Queensland share in the maintenance of a dingo fence along a part of their western boundary.

River Murray Commission

The most prominent joint enterprises, however, involve permanent facilities and an elaborate process of handling their construction, operation, and maintenance. The oldest such enterprise in Australia is the River Murray Commission.[9] Both because of the importance of the Murray-Darling river system to arid Australia[10] and because of the excellent record the commission has achieved since it was founded in 1915, it is generally well known, and not a great deal needs to be said about it here. It is enough to point out that the Murray, the Darling, and the tributary Murrumbidgee constitute the

[9] See F. Burke Sheeran, "Australia's River Murray Agreement and Commission," *State Government*, XXXII (Spring 1959), 128–33; see also Hill, *Water into Gold*, Chapter XX and *passim*.

[10] The Murray-Darling river combination extends 2,310 miles from the sea to its headwaters; it constitutes one of the largest river systems in the world, ranking with the Niger and Volga.

one great inland river system in Australia and the only inter-state river of any importance. The system drains the rich agricultural areas of New South Wales and Victoria and constitutes the only stream of any magnitude—and the main source of water—in South Australia, through which it flows four hundred miles to the sea. The problem with the Murray is not so much flood control, as with rivers in the United States, but the opposite—preserving and achieving maximum utilization of what little water falls in the basin. The average rainfall there is only 17 inches a year, compared with an annual average of about 50 inches in the Tennessee Valley, for example. Three times since gauging was begun at Swan Hill, Victoria, in 1909, the Murray has ceased to flow alto-gether—in 1914, 1915, and 1923. In April 1915, indeed, "no flow was recorded for the whole month—the river being reduced to a chain of water holes."[11] Although it forms the boundary between New South Wales and Victoria, legally the Murray lies within New South Wales. As vital as water is in Australia, such a situation was bound to produce interstate conflict. Almost from its discovery by the explorers Hamilton Hume and William Hovell in 1824, the Murray was the subject of controversy between the colonies. The river was first used for navigation, and for a long while this was its only use. At one time, after paddle steamers based in South Aus-tralia began to ply the river in 1853, trade by boat amounted to more than £1,100,000 a year.[12] The river trade helped greatly to open up large areas of the country upstream for settlement, however, and it was not long before irrigation became more important than navigation, especially to New South Wales and Victoria. Inevitably, the three states began to quarrel. By 1890, each felt that its best interests were

[11] River Murray Commission, *The Work of the River Murray Commission* (1954), p. 37.
[12] Douglas Pike, "South Australia: A Historical Sketch," in *Introducing South Australia* (Melbourne, 1958), p. 15.

being threatened by activities being conducted along the Murray by the other two. South Australia visualized that the river would dry up before it got to her border as an ever-increasing number of irrigation schemes were launched up-river. New South Wales objected to Victorian "water hogs" and "water pirates," and "Victoria sturdily upheld that as her snow-mountains contributed at least four-fifths of the water, she could use as much as she wanted"—and she did so! For a good many years, the three states bickered among themselves about the ownership and use of the Murray. There were "unending royal commissions and interstate commissions and propositions, but no sooner did one State advance a plan than it was promptly stone-walled by the other two. . . . The situation was laughable: New South Wales owned the Murray, Victoria adopted it, and South Australia cried for it."[13] At one stage, intercolonial war did not seem impossible. In the event, however, nothing happened. Not even any litigation was initiated. The three states merely remained obstructionist toward one another, and any effective solution to the conflict seemed completely beyond reach.

With the adoption of the Commonwealth Constitution in 1901, the Commonwealth acquired an interest in the controversy as a result of having been granted power over navigation, and for a while it appeared that something might be done from that quarter. During the Fourth Parliament (1910-1913) a motion was made urging specific amendment of the Constitution to bring the Murray and its tributaries under federal control, but it was withdrawn in the belief that the Inter-State Commission would eventually take action on the problem. That was an ill-founded belief; it was not long before the Inter-State Commission ceased to function at all. And the situation on the Murray went from bad to worse.

It was not until the year of the terrible drought of 1914,

---

[13] The phrases of Sir Henry Parkes, premier of New South Wales, quoted in Hill, *Water into Gold*, pp. 109, 262.

when the river virtually disappeared[14] that the states finally reached agreement on a course of action satisfactory to them all. The Prime Minister of the Commonwealth and the premiers of the three states came to a meeting of the minds first, and the River Murray Agreement, which they all accepted, was later ratified by the four parliaments. The commission created by the agreement went into operation in 1915. It consists of four commissioners—one representing each of the governments—appointed for five-year terms. The commission is charged with controlling the economic use of the river for navigation and irrigation. It has the authority to construct and maintain works, but in actual practice it confines itself to recommending construction, leaving construction and maintenance to the states. The costs of construction are shared by the four governments equally, whereas maintenance costs are borne by the three states alone. The principal works constructed so far are the famous Hume Dam, which is the largest man-made water storage area in the southern hemisphere with its capacity of 2.5 million acre-feet, and the Lake Victoria storage areas.

In addition to fostering the construction of works, the commission operates the dams and locks once they have been built; collects tolls from ships that use the locks; conducts antierosion activities along the banks of the river and its tributaries; makes quality, salinity, and siltation tests; and continually studies the river and its use to assure that it makes its full contribution to Australian development. There has recently been pressure for the commission to add flood control measures to its activities, including snagging and levee development, but so far the commission has not undertaken such projects.

[14] In Ernestine Hill's felicitous words, "New South Wales, Victoria and South Australia, with their quarrelling over the boundary river, resembled nothing so much as neighbors arguing over the fence, and the Murray, like the chestnuts of Aesop, in 1914 . . . slipped between their fingers. The moral found its mark." *Water into Gold*, p. 185.

In 1923, the agreement was amended to provide for the precedence of irrigation works over navigation, and perhaps the commission's greatest accomplishment has been the way it has allocated water to the three states. The agreement stipulates a minimum monthly flow in normal years and a fixed proportion to be made in drought years. In operation, these arrangements have worked very smoothly. In recognition of the growing need for water as the Australian economy develops, the commission has recently begun to plan for a vast expansion of its facilities. Sir Thomas Playford first suggested the idea of a new dam on the lower reaches of the Murray, and the commission was asked to investigate the feasibility of the proposal and report back to the four governments. In October 1961 the commission announced its endorsement of the project and made a formal recommendation to the states to that effect. The recommendation has since been accepted by all the party governments, and construction of a new dam at Chowilla, just over the border in South Australia, is under way. Legislation will be necessary to amend the River Murray Agreement to provide for the Chowilla Dam and the distribution of its waters, but pending action by the states, the commission is going ahead with plans for construction. When the dam is completed, it will be at the same time the most expensive ever to be built in Australia and the largest by far, almost doubling the capacity of the Hume Dam. The Commonwealth will pay one quarter of the costs, and the states will share the remainder equally.

Perhaps no governmental agency in Australia is as respected as the River Murray Commission. The extent of the states' satisfaction with its operations can be judged from the fact that no official criticism has been made of the commission in all the years of its existence. Instead, the states have followed the commission's recommendations without hesitation. Nor has any of the states failed to meet in full its financial obligations under the agreement or to cooperate in construction and maintenance as requested by the commission. The reasons for this evident faith in the commission are not hard to find. For one thing, from the time the commission was established, the states have been regarded by the commissioners as the majority stockholders, so to speak, the Commonwealth as the minority interest. Except for one full-time employee—an executive engineer—the commission has functioned through state officers and agencies. The Commonwealth has provided secretarial and accounting services, and its commissioner serves as chairman, but it has not sought to assert undue pressure. The states have thus felt that the commission is their instrument, to be used as their needs and interests require. And the commissioners themselves have been chosen to inspire confidence. The states have seen to it that the commissioners have been persons of distinction and ability, active and knowledgeable in state conservation and irrigation activities. The chairman of the Water Conservation and Irrigation Commission of New South Wales has served as that state's representative on the River Murray Commission, and the South Australia and Victoria representatives are usually the same kind of professionally oriented men. As a result, their decisions have been made in engineering terms rather than in political. And they have been careful to remember that their role is recommendatory, leaving the final decision up to the state parliaments.

Interstate cooperation through the River Murray Agreement and Commission has thus been the key to the solution of the old problem of controlling the Murray's waters, a key, fortunately for Australia, which has fitted the lock of Australian development perfectly. All three states, and the Commonwealth as a whole as well, have benefitted from the commission's activities. For in Ernestine Hill's words, the commission has done nothing less than keep the Murray "safe for posterity."[15] The commission has not only served

15 *Ibid.*, p. 263.

admirably the purposes for which it was created; it has had also a number of important side effects. Working together on commission business has brought the water and irrigation agencies of the three states into friendly and helpful relationships in several additional areas, and this spirit of cooperation has spread to other state departments and agencies. Thus, New South Wales and Victoria share equally in the distribution of the output of a 500,000 kilowatt hydroelectric generating station at the Hume Dam, and the three state forestry departments have worked out several joint enterprises in connection with lands adjacent to the river. But probably the greatest impact the River Murray Commission has had outside its own field of concern is the model it offered New South Wales, Victoria, and the Commonwealth for putting the Snowy Mountains Scheme into effect after World War II.

Snowy Mountains Council

The Snowy Mountains, the highest part of the Australian continent, give rise to three rivers—the Snowy, the Murrumbidgee, and the Murray. The Snowy's waters have always been wasted, because they flow southeast through already well-watered country straight into the Tasman Sea. The Snowy Mountains Scheme is a plan to save those waters by diverting them and those of the Snowy's tributary, the Eucumbene, into the Murray and Murrumbidgee, which flow westward toward South Australia. The works of the scheme will catch the Snowy and Eucumbene waters before they leave high elevations and divert them, through long transmountain tunnels, into the westward-flowing rivers. In traveling through the mountains, they will fall more than 2,500 feet and in the process will generate electricity at a number of power stations along the way. The scheme thus will not only vastly increase the quantity of water available for irrigation in the Murray Valley but also provide a tremendous new source of electric power production. It is the greatest single engineering project ever undertaken in Australia, and one of the largest in the world. It involves an area of nearly 3,000 square miles, and when completed, it will permit the development of some 1,000 square miles of western land not now in cultivation and will support an estimated increased agricultural population of 150,000 persons. It involves the ultimate construction of nine major dams and a great many smaller ones, approximately 100 miles of mountain tunnels, ten power stations, and over 90 miles of aqueducts to catch little mountain streams and rivulets that would otherwise be lost to the reservoirs and tunnels. It will provide 2.5 million kilowatts of peak-load electric power and an estimated 2 million acre-feet of water a year. Its cost will be about £400,000,000.[16]

The scheme is being developed as a Commonwealth project by a Commonwealth agency, the Snowy Mountains Authority, at Commonwealth expense.[17] It was originally undertaken as an exercise of the Commonwealth's defense power. It might have been developed quite differently, of course, had the states been able to agree on a course of action in the first place. For more than forty years before the Commonwealth finally moved to undertake the present project, proposal after proposal had been made, first by New South Wales and then by Victoria, for some kind of joint action to develop the irrigation and hydroelectric potential of the Snowy River. But as in the early development of the River Murray, the states never could agree on an approach. So the years went by, and nothing was done. As Australia began to plan her postwar development, however, further delay began to seem intolerable, even to the states. Finally, in 1946, the premier of Victoria urged

16 For an illustrated and well-written description of the scheme, see Australian Publicity Council, *Liquid Gold—Australia* (Melbourne, 1961), pp. 114–44.
17 Appropriations to the authority are treated as loans; revenue to repay the loans is obtained by the authority from the bulk sale of electricity to the states. Water for irrigation is made available to the states without charge.

the Prime Minister to consider developing the Snowy as a Commonwealth project. "The diversion of the Snowy River into the Murray," he wrote, "would undoubtedly be a national undertaking which would be of very great benefit, and [the Victorian] Government is of the opinion that the whole of the project . . . including hydroelectric development, could well be undertaken by the Commonwealth Government as a national work."[18] The Prime Minister agreed that the Commonwealth might look into the matter, and in 1947 the preliminary findings of its investigation were reported to the Premiers' Conference. The premiers promptly resolved that the Commonwealth and the states of Victoria and New South Wales should "agree to the diversion of the Snowy River Waters into the River Murray and to the commencement of construction as soon as possible."[19] Subsequently, a group representing each of the three governments was appointed to prepare detailed plans for the project, and its recommendations were accepted by the Premiers' Conference in 1949. Before the year was out, the Commonwealth had set up the Snowy Mountains Authority, appointed the commissioners to man it, charged them with the responsibility for planning and constructing the project, let the first contracts, and actually broken sod for the first bit of construction. By 1962, the scheme was about half completed.

In all this, the states seem to have had no part, save that of acquiescence. Thus the scheme is not modeled exactly upon the River Murray Commission, under which the states themselves are the constructing authorities. Rather, it is like the Muscle Shoals Project and its successor, the Tennessee Valley Authority, in the United States. But the scheme was not developed without the states in mind. From the first the states were involved in its planning, as of course they had to

[18] Hon. John Cain, in State of Victoria, *Snowy Mountains Hydro-Electric Agreements Bill . . . 18th March, 1958* (Melbourne, 1958), p. 2. The letter was cited as a supporting document.
[19] *Ibid.*

be. The Snowy Mountains, after all, lie in New South Wales, and both New South Wales and Victoria have rights in the water being diverted. Moreover, the electricity commissions of the two states will buy most of the electricity,[20] and the states' irrigation authorities will control the increased flow of water. Even without these factors, the theory and practice of Australian federalism would still have demanded participation by the states in the scheme, for the feeling was widespread at first that the Commonwealth, in responding so quickly to the call for action on the project, had acted unconstitutionally in setting up the Snowy Mountains Authority on a unilateral basis, and that by so doing it had invaded "the field of internal improvement hitherto the domain of the States."[21] The Commonwealth would have had trouble had it not sought to involve the states in a meaningful and significant way in carrying out the project. And in fact it did recognize the importance of the states' interests and did not neglect them. The same committee that reported detailed plans to the Premiers' Conference in 1949 also submitted the draft of an intergovernmental agreement dealing with the handling of the completed works. The sections of the agreement concerning distribution of water immediately became the subject of heated discussion between the states, however, and the problems raised therein were not settled for nearly ten years. The agreement was not accepted by all the parties concerned until 1958, going into effect on January 2, 1959.

When it became apparent that it would be a long time before the argument over water distribution would be settled, an Interim Advisory Council was appointed to bring the states into the picture. Between July 1953, when it was established,

[20] Some of the power produced is reserved under the scheme to meet the needs of the Commonwealth government, but as far as can be foreseen, this will be a small proportion of the total to be made available. The remainder of the output will be divided between the two states, one-third for Victoria and two-thirds for New South Wales.

[21] Campbell, *Australian State Public Finance*, p. 112.

and 1958, when it held its last meeting, it met twenty-two times. Its formal meetings were "supplemented by numerous and extensive discussions between officers of the Commonwealth, the Snowy Mountains Authority, and the States. As a consequence, the work of the Authority [was] subject to constant review by technical officers of the States' electrical and water conservation authorities."[22] The states were thus included at an early stage, and they took full advantage of their opportunity.

Part VI of the agreement called for the creation of a permanent interstate body to be known as the Snowy Mountains Council, which would have responsibility for operating and maintaining the completed works.[23] From the first, it was taken for granted that the authority's—i.e., the Commonwealth's—role would be primarily that of construction and that the states would be given the job of operation and maintenance. When plans were made for a vehicle to be employed here, the River Murray Commission seemed to be an appropriate model, and was followed. Although the council is still only in its infancy, it is already apparent that the model was a good one.

The composition of the council is somewhat more complicated than that of the River Murray Commission because of the different interests that must be involved. The Snowy Mountains Agreement calls for a council of eight members, two from the Commonwealth, two from the Snowy Mountains Authority, and two from each state. The agreement also provides for the appointment of deputy members to attend when the appointed members are unable to do so. In practice, the deputies attend meetings along with the members themselves. The Commonwealth appointed the perma-

22 Snowy Mountains Hydro-Electric Agreements Bill, p. 4.

23 The bulk of the agreement deals with the construction of supplementary works; the control, diversion, storage, and distribution of water; the protection of catchment areas; the generation, supply, and assignment of electricity; and the assessment of costs.

nent Secretary of the Department of National Development and the Director General of the Department of Works as its representatives. The former serves as chairman of the council, and a member of his staff has been designated secretary of the council. By the terms of the agreement, the commissioner of the Snowy Mountains Authority and an associate commissioner of his choice represent the authority. Both states have appointed the chairmen of their electricity and water and irrigation commissions to the council. Like the River Murray Commission, the council has thus been assured since the outset that the government officers who are most concerned with its work are drawn into the development of policy controlling it. Unlike members of the Murray Commission, however, council members are not appointed for a specific term of office; they serve at the appointing government's pleasure.

The council has developed the habit of holding six to eight meetings a year. During the fiscal year of 1962, for example, it held five meetings.[24] The agreement provides in some detail how the council shall conduct its business. Meetings are to be held on the call of the chairman and at such other times as any two members may request, thus giving each state in effect an opportunity to have the council called into session. In any case, there shall be at least one meeting every six months. No resolution may be adopted unless a representative of each of the governments and of the Snowy Mountains Authority is present and has a chance to vote; "in the event of an equality of votes, the presiding member shall have a casting as well as a deliberative vote."[25] When the council is serving in its capacity as advisor to the authority, one of the authority members—the associate commissioner—may not vote. Should council decisions not be unanimous, the agreement requires

[24] Commonwealth of Australia, *Snowy Mountains Council, Fourth Annual Report . . . 1st July 1961 to 30th June 1962* (Canberra, 1962), p. 2.
[25] Snowy Mountains Hydro-Electric Agreement, Part VI, Clause 18 (4).

that the views of the minority shall be recorded if it so requests. Finally, the council is required to report annually to the three governments on its activities and to keep the Minister for National Development informed of any decisions it makes in the exercise of its function of direction and control.

The council has three distinct functions. Its primary job is to operate and maintain the works constructed by the Snowy Mountains Authority; this function includes allocating electric power loads to the generating stations. (So far only three power stations have come under the council's control.) The agreement does not leave the council free to organize the operation of the completed works as it sees fit, however. It requires that they be operated by the state electricity commissions and the authority, under the council's direction and control. What the council has therefore done is to work through an Operations Engineers' Committee, which consists of an operations engineer appointed by the Snowy Mountains Authority and two assistant operations engineers, one appointed by each of the state electricity commissions. The council passes its directions along to the committee for implementation, and the committee in turn reports regularly to the council and advises it on operations matters. In 1962, the council decided to ask the authority to lend one of its staff members to serve as executive engineer of the council. The authority did so, and this is now a fulltime position, controlling the staff that operates and maintains the headquarters and also all manning personnel.[26] The executive engineer and his staff carry out the committee's instructions and link the council with the state electricity commissions, whose salaried personnel are in actual charge of the power stations. And as the executive engineer is himself an authority em-

[26] *Snowy Mountains Council, Fourth Annual Report*, p. 3. This particular report contains a full description of the council's working arrangements and should be read in its entirety.

ployee, he also serves as liaison between the council and the Snowy Mountains Authority, which continues to play an important role even after construction has been completed. It makes engineering and clerical help available to the Operations Engineers' Committee and supplies the wages of staff to man the power stations. It carries out maintenance on behalf of the council; it provides support services, such as transport and snow clearing; it performs accounting and financial services; and it gives advice on all hydraulic aspects of the council's work. Without such extensive cooperation, the council itself would be forced to provide all those services at considerable expense to the three contracting governments.

To date, of course, since the number of completed works is still small, the second function of the council, direction and control, has not assumed great importance. More important has been its advisory function. According to the agreement (Part VI, Clause 19-2-B), the council shall advise on "the co-ordination of the works carried out or to be carried out by the authority with the works carried out or to be carried out by the states for (a) the generation and transmission of electricity and (b) irrigation." In carrying out this instruction, the council serves as a guarantee that the basic responsibility both for producing electric power and for supplying water will continue to lie with the state governments, and that the authority's projects will supplement rather than replace state projects. Although the authority's works will greatly increase the flow in the Murray and its tributaries, the regulation and disposition of the water therein remain with the states. The council serves to remind both the authority and the states of these elemental facts and is a tool that both can use to make the adjustments that will increasingly be demanded as the scheme nears completion. The council is not limited to advising on coordination, however. The agreement (Clause 19-3-a, b, c, d) also gives it the power to study and report to the participating governments on a number of other topics: "the nature, order, sequence and rate of construction of works of the Authority"; "matters affecting the States in respect of the diversion, storage and release of waters by the Authority"; "matters affecting the States in respect of the generation, transmission, allocation and use of the electricity generated by the Authority"; and "matters affecting the States in respect of catchment areas." On all these matters, the council's concern is the states and their citizens and the effect of the authority's operations on both. It is in a sense the states' joint protection against the authority's power and prestige. A good example of the council at work in this capacity is the case of the property owners in the Lower Tumut Valley. The Tumut River project was one of the first to be tackled by the authority, and as soon as the work was completed and additional water began to flow downstream, there were complaints from landholders in the lower valley that the project had caused them damage, loss of income, and inconvenience. The complaints were referred to the council, which then undertook to study them from every point of view. Its conclusion, reported to the states (in this case, only New South Wales was immediately concerned) and the authority, was that the complaints were justified. The report recommended that the authority, in conjunction with the New South Wales Water Conservation and Irrigation Commission, take "action to improve the river channel by de-snagging and by protecting the banks from erosion." This was done, and in a number of cases property access was improved by building bridges. On the advice of the authority the council agreed to purchase one especially low-lying property from its owner.[27] To date the major impact of the authority's work—and thus of the council's investigations and reports—has been in New South Wales. Beginning in 1962, however, major construction projects were begun on the Snowy-Murray development on the Victorian side of the

[27] See *ibid.*, p. 10, for the story in full.

Great Dividing Range, and adjustments by the council will probably be necessary in Victoria as well.

Finally, the council has the power to make specific determinations with regard to the production and sale of electricity from the authority's works. The agreement sets the basic pattern for both production and sale to the states, but it gives the council the authority to vary the rates and periods of production if it is satisfied that savings would be made by so doing and that the interests of none of the parties to the agreement, nor of their instrumentalities, would be prejudiced thereby. Indeed, making these determinations will increasingly become one of the most important aspects of the council's work.

As the River Murray Commission demonstrates, much of the long-term success of the Snowy Mountains Council will depend on the degree of rapport it creates with its several members. The agreement itself requires a certain amount of contact, and in operation the council has assiduously developed other avenues. The agreement, for example, provides (Part VI, Clause 20) that the authority shall keep the council informed about "the nature and costs of all proposed works . . . [;] the sequence, rate and progress of construction of those works; its proposals for the diversion of waters and the operating procedures [therefor]; the position in respect of the waters held or supposed to be held from time to time in storage under the control of the Authority; [and] all matters which may affect the interests of the States in respect of the use of those waters and in respect of the generation, transmission, allocation and use of the electricity generated by means of the use of those waters." The authority has been careful to comply with those requirements, and as a result the council has from the first had the most cordial relations with it. The fact that the Snowy Mountains Commissioner is a member of the council has been a further guarantee of harmony between the two bodies. The agreement also assures cooperation between the council and the states by providing for state membership on the council. But the council itself has gone considerably further than that minimum requirement assures. In every action it has taken, it has actively sought the advice and counsel of the state officers and agencies concerned and has usually followed it, so that the states have developed a feeling of respect for and confidence in the council. For example, the council has developed liaison with the irrigation authorities of the two states. The council notifies the states daily as to the amount of water released from the power stations under its control. The states have therefore been able to plan new irrigation areas more efficiently than they otherwise would.[28] Finally, because a member of the staff of the Commonwealth Department of National Development is secretary of the council, and because the Commonwealth representative of that department chairs the council, a clear and direct avenue of contact exists between the council and the Minister of National Development and extends through him to the Commonwealth government as a whole.

The Snowy Mountains Council is still too young for anyone to be over-sanguine about its success, although it has proceeded so far in an atmosphere of extraordinary harmony and good will. Two sources of possible future trouble have already been identified, and as the scheme draws nearer to completion, others may appear. The anomalous position of South Australia has posed the first problem. Although New South Wales and Victoria are the major beneficiaries of the scheme, and as such are the only formal parties to the agreement, South Australia stands to gain as well, because improved conservation and storage upstream will result in a greater volume of water downstream, especially in dry periods. More-

[28] See *ibid.*, p. 4; see also Commonwealth of Australia, *Snowy Mountains Council, Third Annual Report . . . 1st July 1960 to 30th June 1961* (Canberra, 1961), p. 3.

over, the general flow of the Murray will be appreciably increased, so the number of dry periods should be considerably reduced. In the light of these facts, the agreement was amended in 1958 to provide that when conditions are normal, New South Wales and Victoria are each entitled to half the water diverted from the Snowy into the Murray (after deductions for storage upstream), but that during a drought, when a period of restriction has been declared by the River Murray Commission, the whole of the water resources under that commission's control are to be shared by New South Wales, Victoria, and South Australia, under the terms of the River Murray Agreement. In these circumstances, South Australia will obtain a share of the Snowy's waters. Thus South Australia is a party in fact to the scheme, if not a party in law to the council, which will be coming more and more to the fore as works are completed and turned over to it. The problems that may arise cannot be foreseen with precision. It will probably take a year of drought to bring them to the fore. Given South Australia's long history of dissension, however, it would seem safe to predict that problems of some kind will arise there to plague the council in the future.

The other possible problem involves the relationship between the River Murray Commission and the Snowy Mountains Council. The Snowy Mountains Agreement was correlated from the outset with the River Murray Agreement. The latter is mentioned in the whereases at the very beginning of the Snowy Mountains Agreement as well as in Part III, in connection with the diversion and discharge of water from the scheme's works. And when the River Murray Agreement was amended in 1958 to deal with South Australia's position, the right of the River Murray Commission "to define the rights to water in the River Murray and its tributaries" was specifically affirmed. The additional water made available for irrigation by the scheme will be stored, however, in the Hume Reservoir and in the Blowering Reservoir, to be built by New

South Wales for the commission. The Hume Dam was developed to a capacity of 2.5 million acre-feet, in fact, largely to accommodate the additional water from the Snowy. Thus the impact of the scheme on the commission's activities will steadily become greater. No immediate problems seem to exist as a result of this development, but as new works come under the council's aegis, some effective liaison between the council and the commission may well become necessary. It is possible that the River Murray Commission will one day become a full partner in the deliberations and activities of the council.

Whether the Snowy Mountains Authority will be continued when construction is finished in 1975 or whether it will be adapted to another purpose[29] or dropped altogether will have a bearing on the future of the council, for the authority now bears a large part of the council's expenses and performs a good deal of work for it. Finally, it is too early to tell how effective the council's *modus operandi* will be. Its role so far has been a fairly limited one. There is no assurance that its operations will always be as smooth as everyone seems to expect. Certainly the procedures that have been worked out to date are very different from those in the River Murray Agreement, which has been phenomenally successful in operation. There is some feeling that the Snowy Agreement may be less successful, as might be expected of "a compromise between Governments which have different ideas of how and by whom things should be done."[30] As the years go by, the council will be subjected to conflicting pressures from the two main interests concerned in the scheme. The irrigation commissions and their constituents will obviously want water released in the summer when the need is greatest; the elec-

---

[29] A number of suggestions that the authority be turned into a body like the United States Bureau of Reclamation have already been advanced. There is no such agency at present on the Commonwealth level in Australia.

[30] W. J. Mibus, Minister of Water Supply, Victoria, to author, January 20, 1960.

tricity commissions and their constituents will argue for the winter, when demand for electric power is heaviest. The council must resolve the conflict as a regular part of its duties. For a while there is little doubt that irrigation will have first priority; the context of the whole scheme points in this direction. Should the situation change, however, and priority be demanded for electric power production, the council will be caught squarely in the middle. The real test of its strength and viability can then be expected.

It should also be mentioned perhaps that the council under present arrangements will never have its own personnel whose loyalty is first to the council. Using the employees of the authority and of the state electricity commissions creates special problems of management—or may do so in the future. The River Murray Commission, with fewer and simpler works, and thus fewer persons involved in its operations, provides no guidelines here at all.

The consensus in Australia, however, is that the council will work and that it will achieve a record as a device for interstate action as good as that of the River Murray Commission. Certainly, the area of its concern is of vast importance to the states involved and to the entire Commonwealth. Neither the states nor the Commonwealth Government underestimate that importance, and the continued support of both levels can be assumed in the years ahead.

A project with as many ramifications as the Snowy Mountains Scheme could hardly help having side effects, some of which involve interstate cooperation. The cooperation between New South Wales and Victoria in the Corryong-Khancoban-Geehi area, high in the Snowy Mountains, is perhaps the most dramatic case in point. When the work on the scheme was begun, Corryong was a remote mountain village in Victoria, the only one of any size in the entire area. The Snowy Mountains Authority established the township of Khancoban just across the border in New South Wales to house workers on the Snowy-Geehi Tunnel, the Geehi Dam, the Murray I Project, and related construction jobs. By 1961, the population there had grown to over 1,000 persons. It is expected to reach about 3,000 by 1965 and then to drop off substantially after construction in the area is completed around 1970. The need for services—particularly health and education services—for the workers and their families thus developed almost overnight and within a few years will have disappeared again. Meanwhile, however, it had to be met—promptly and adequately. Under arrangements worked out by the Snowy Mountains Authority and by the Upper Murray Regional Committee (an informal group representing the various interests in the area other than the authority), a number of cooperative interstate services have been worked out. All the residents of the Geehi region are serviced in the first instance by the Corryong District Hospital in Victoria. In the event of an emergency—an epidemic, for example—patients will be sent to the Cooma District Hospital in New South Wales. The Corryong Branch of the North-Western Ambulance Service (Victoria) built a new branch station to provide ambulance services for patients throughout the area. The Victoria Health Department provided an infant-welfare service to the township of Khancoban. An infant-welfare sister whose mobile circuit is based at Corryong visits Khancoban on alternate Wednesday afternoons. The New South Wales Education Department provided a primary school at Khancoban, and the primary facilities at Corryong were expanded. Secondary school facilities for all the residents in the region were made available at Corryong. Bus transport, subsidized by New South Wales, was provided to and from Corryong. All this was done with a minimum of fuss about costs. With the help of the authority and the Upper Murray Regional Committee, the two states simply approached the health and education problems of the region jointly and worked out solutions, with no preconceived notions about

who should do what. The arrangements are admittedly only
for a short time, but the fact that they were made so quickly
and are proving so satisfactory in operation is a reflection of
the acceptance of interstate cooperation as a useful tool of
government and administration in the area.

Another direct result of the scheme as far as interstate
relations are concerned is the interconnection of the New
South Wales and Victoria electricity systems for peak-load
purposes. Considerable savings for both states will thus be
possible, and the overall reliability of both systems will be
vastly increased by the agreement to pool spare plant. Having
a pattern of interconnection may be even more important in a
future age of nuclear power. In the words of the 1958-1959
Report of the State Electricity Commission of Victoria: "This
line provides an important operating link between the two
State transmission systems, for until now there has been
provision only for a quite limited interchange at Hume.
Clearly in an emergency there is considerable advantage in
this facility for more extensive interchange. Moreover, the
formal agreement between the two State Electricity Commissions legislating for the interchange provides for the operation of the most economical plant available at any time and
for the sharing of overall savings in cost equally between the
two Commissions. This is to the mutual benefit of the two
States."[31]

Dumaresq-Barwon Border Rivers Commission

The final instance of formal interstate cooperation that has
developed in Australia involves joint action between New
South Wales and Queensland along the part of their common
boundary that is formed by a number of continuous rivers,
variously called the Dumaresq or Severn, the Macintyre, and

[31] State Electricity Commission of Victoria, *40th Annual Report 1958–59*,
pp. 8–9.

the Barwon. These streams are fed from catchments in both states, and tributaries flow into the main rivers from both sides of the border. The development and use of the water resources of the rivers, which, like the Murray's, are scarce enough at best, obviously required the joint efforts of the two states, but only since World War II have the efforts been begun. The New South Wales government initiated discussions with Queensland, and in remarkably short order agreement was reached as to what needed to be done, and how and by whom it ought to be handled. That agreement was embodied in acts passed simultaneously by the Queensland and New South Wales parliaments in 1947. As their agent to carry out the terms of the agreement, the states created the Dumaresq-Barwon Border Rivers Commission. There are three commissioners, chosen for five-year terms, one each appointed by the governors of New South Wales and Queensland, and the third, who serves as chairman and who must not be a person in government, appointed jointly by the premiers of the two states.[32] The Commonwealth is not in any way involved in this commission or its work, which makes it unique among interstate commissions in Australia. The commission's duties are fairly technical. The agreement provides in detail for the distribution and use of the rivers' waters, and the commission is charged with arranging with the two states for the construction, maintenance, operation, and control of the weirs and dams necessary to maintain maximum flow. It also sees to it that accurate and regular measurements of water flow are taken at stream-gaging stations operated by the states, so that the terms of the agreement with regard to distribution can be strictly adhered to. Six weirs have so far come under the commission's jurisdiction, and it is currently

[32] There is a complicated provision in the agreement for the appointment of the third member in the event the two premiers cannot agree on a name, but in fact it has never been used. It provides for a panel of names to be drawn up by the two premiers and submitted to the chief justice either of New South Wales or of Queensland (by turns), who makes the selection.

considering the construction of dams at three points on tributary streams. The commission is also constantly alert to the need for investigation into hydrologic aspects of the river basin and usually has one or more projects underway.[33] All the costs of the commission's activities are shared equally by the two states.

There have been virtually no problems in the commission's short lifetime. The rivers involved are far from great ones, and once the agreement had been accepted, the problems of managing the use of their waters have been routine. The commission ordinarily meets only once a year and then confines its discussions largely to matters of engineering. Most of the actual work has of course been performed by the states, which have given their wholehearted support to the commission from the beginning.

Although the role of the commission in its limited capacity is not an unimportant one, either to the two states involved or to interstate cooperation generally, it may be that the example it has provided for additional interstate cooperation has been even more important. Like the River Murray Commission, it has led directly to additional instances of cooperation between the parties to it. Its meetings have brought water conservation and irrigation officers from the two states together regularly for over fifteen years, and so well have they come to know each other that there is a great deal of minor cooperation in administrative matters going on all the time. Even more, their rapport has led to several more formal arrangements. The Dumaresq-Barwon Border Rivers Water Advisory Board was established in 1957 to represent landholders along the rivers for the purpose of securing their close cooperation with the work of the Border Rivers Commission. Under the constitution of the board, a representative of the Queensland Irrigation and Water Supply Com-

[33] Parliament of New South Wales, *Report of Dumaresq-Barwon Rivers Commission for the Year Ended 30th June, 1960* (1960), pp. 1-2.

mission presides at the annual meetings, and any matter relating to water use in the basin may be raised for discussion. The water and irrigation commissions of the two states drew up an agreement for collaboration in the investigation of underground water in the alluvial flats on both sides of the border rivers. The bulk of the work under the agreement is being carried out by Queensland, but technical control and costs are shared by the two states. And in July 1958 an interdepartmental Border Rivers Interstate Levee Committee was set up to study proposals for levee licenses on any of the border rivers and to make recommendations on these to the states. Like the parent Rivers Commission, the Levee Committee has been well received from the first and has considerably improved the handling of requests for levees.

Formal interstate arrangements have become very common in Australia, and at least by the small group of government officials directly involved in them, they are regarded as important and are entered into with enthusiasm. They have demonstrated their utility time and time again in helping to overcome the difficulties of a federal system in operation and have added appreciably to the strength of state government in Australia in the process. Because of their record in the past, they will very likely be used increasingly in the future. Already a number of areas where joint action seems possible have been identified, and as interstate cooperation in general grows in Australia, a further expansion in the number of interstate enterprises is bound to take place.

Chapter 6 UNIFORM LAW

On the basis of bulk, the chief product of the increasing number of informal and formal relations between state officials in Australia is administrative cooperation—cooperation in program planning and implementation. It is administrators, after all, who most frequently attend meetings and who thus have the opportunity to develop contacts that may lead to joint enterprises. But administrative cooperation, however important it is to the successful functioning of a federal system, does not assure that the states will all take the same approach in attacking common problems that can be solved satisfactorily only by uniform legislation in force in all the states. Indeed, perhaps the most difficult problem in every federal system is that of achieving uniform action where it is necessary while maintaining the degree of diversity that is felt to be desirable in a free society. Variations in state laws, and the conflict that resulted from them, did not matter so much in Australia (or in any of the other federal systems in the world, for that matter) when there were fewer people and when transportation and communication facilities were so primitive that integrated communities did not develop. Differences in state law did not then greatly handicap national progress. As population increased, however, and as the citizens of Australia began to draw together into a single economic and social unit, the lack of uniform laws in a number of areas began to grow serious, and Australia discovered that, her federal system notwithstanding, interdependence demanded uniform state legislation if the nation were to develop to its maximum.

Uniform Law in the United States and Canada

The same discovery had been made earlier in the United States, where the number of separate units of government was large and where the area held by the Supreme Court to be reserved for state action—and thus foreclosed to action by the national government—was extensive, to say the least, especially in the years just after the Civil War. The American Bar Association, which was formed in 1878, dedicated itself in part to securing "uniformity of legislation . . . throughout the nation"[1] and so helped pave the way for action. Largely as a result of the association's efforts, what soon came to be known as the National Conference of Commissioners on Uniform State Laws came into being in 1892. The object of the conference is to promote legislative uniformity in those fields of law in which uniformity seems desirable and practicable. This it does by carefully preparing model uniform acts to be recommended to the states for adoption. Since it was founded, the conference has drawn every state in the Union into its activities, and its accomplishments have been many.[2] Of the eighty-odd recommendations for uniform legislation and the thirty model acts prepared under the conference's auspices, a significant number, particularly in the fields of commercial law, civil procedure, and property law, have been adopted by many of the states. Although the conference will probably never achieve total adoption of its recommendations, even in the areas it feels to be critical, it nevertheless constitutes a powerful force constantly at work in behalf of uniformity, without whose leadership there would be far less achievement in the United States than there is.

[1] The Constitution of the American Bar Association, quoted in W. Brooke Graves, *Uniform State Action* (Chapel Hill, 1934), p. 33. Part II of this book is devoted to uniform legislation, and the entire book remains an indispensable landmark study of the broad subject indicated by its title.

[2] See *The Book of the States, 1960–61* (Chicago, 1960), pp. 84–87, for a list of the uniform laws recommended by the conference and adopted by the states since the conference started to function.

Canada also saw the need to provide some device by which her provinces could more effectively act together in the areas assigned to them by the British North America Act, and in 1918, the Canadian Bar Association, following the example of the United States, instigated the establishment of the Conference of Commissioners on Uniformity of Legislation in Canada.[3] For some while, the province of Quebec did not participate in the work of the conference, but since 1942 representatives from Quebec and occasionally of the government of the province have attended its meetings. "The primary object of the Conference is to promote uniformity of legislation throughout Canada or the provinces in which uniformity may be found to be practicable by whatever means are suitable to that end." The conference functions much like its American counterpart, with which it has worked closely since the beginning. "At the annual meetings of the Conference, consideration is given to those branches of the law in respect of which it is desirable and practicable to secure uniformity. . . . [M]atters for the consideration of the Conference may be brought forward by a member, the Minister of Justice, the Attorney-General of any province, or the Canadian Bar Association."[4] Complete uniformity across Canada on any subject will be difficult, if not impossible, to attain, because the legal roots and traditions of Quebec are so different from those of the other provinces. Even so, the conference deserves a great deal of credit for its accomplishments, for it has been instrumental in bringing about at least a degree of uniformity in some fifty-four legal areas between many of the provinces other than Quebec.

In both the United States and Canada, other forces as well

[3] The name of the conference first made use of the word "laws" instead of "legislation" in its title. The present name was adopted in 1919. For a full discussion of the conference, see the brochure put out by the conference, *Uniformity of Legislation in Canada—An Outline* (Ottawa, 1949).

[4] *Proceedings of the 42nd Annual Meeting of the Conference of Commissioners on Uniformity of Legislation in Canada* (Ottawa, 1960), p. 12. A full table of titles and adoptions is given on pp. 14–15.

have sought for uniform legislation. The Council of State Governments has been chief among them in the United States, and in Canada the leading groups are the Association of Superintendents of Insurance, whose interests have been particularly directed toward uniform automobile and fire insurance acts in the several provinces, and the Federal-Provincial Committee on Uniformity of Company Law, which has been at work in that area since before World War II and has drafted a uniform act to be submitted to the provinces.

Australian Resistance to Uniform Law

Australia, however, was long in following the pattern set in North America. Until just recently, there was very little conscious uniformity in state law "down under."[5] The idea of uniform law had few friends either among party leaders or among leaders of the bar. It seldom occurred to anyone in either group, in fact, and when it did, it was dismissed as unnecessary, impractical, and undesirable.

It was unnecessary, went the argument, because Australian law has always been fairly uniform. Although six separate systems of state law exist, they have a basic similarity in that, both in spirit and in content, they are all derived from English law. It is the custom in all of the states to seek a British model whenever a new field of legislation is entered, with the result that much state legislation is virtually copied from the English original, even to this day. The Sales of Goods Acts in the states are excellent examples. Moreover, if state officials have learned anything from the many conferences that they have attended through the years, it is the

[5] My concern here is with state law only. The Commonwealth recently exerted its power under the Constitution to make marriage laws uniform by the passage of the Uniform Marriage Act. But the title merely reflects the late exercise of a long dormant Commonwealth power rather than the evolution of a uniform law in a field of state power.

value of interchange of information. Officials soon formed the habit of making copies of legislation available to counterpart officials in other states. Very often the act drawn up for the first time by one of the states is nearly identical to an act it has received from a sister state. The land transfer system now used in all of Australia, the Torrens system, was adopted by all the states from the original South Australian model. And when legislation is being framed, state officers frequently are called upon to give advice to officers in other states, either in person at a conference meeting or by mail or by personal visit, with the result again that many uniform provisions have come to exist. Thus, "uniform legislation," even if not in the American and Canadian sense of the term, already exists in many areas of law in Australia.

More than that, the argument continued, uniform law is impractical. Not only are "the delay and waste of effort involved in securing the passage of a uniform bill through thirteen Houses of Parliament" excessive and needless,[6] but eventual uniformity is an illusion. As Sir Thomas Playford remarked, "it would be far from easy to get all the States to agree to [uniform] legislation. . . . The State legislatures would not consider themselves bound to accept all the ideas [embodied in a draft bill]. Therefore, although we might start off with uniform legislation by the time . . . it passed through the State parliaments, it would be far from uniform. Queensland might amend one clause, South Australia, another, and so on. . . . I am afraid that the State legislatures would take immediate exception if they were told that they must accept a model bill without alteration. . . . I should not be prepared to place model legislation before the South

[6] The words of Prime Minister Curtin in *Convention on Alteration of Constitution*, p. 3. Mr. Curtin referred to thirteen parliaments inasmuch as there are six states with two houses of parliament each, save Queensland, which has a unicameral legislature, and the Commonwealth (which is involved in most uniform law, because it must legislate for the territories), with two houses of its own.

Australian Parliament and insist that it should not be altered."[7] Nor are the reasons for Sir Thomas' pessimism hard to find. The Australian states pride themselves on their long-standing differences, and no one knows the effects of their pride on interstate relations better than Sir Thomas. And his views are shared by others. Many of the state people I interviewed echoed his points almost word for word.

Finally, uniform law for a long time was felt to be undesirable. What would be its effect on the diversity that the Australians prized so much? What did absolute uniformity have to recommend it that accidental uniformity did not have in equal proportions? With no organizations like the conferences in North America to answer such questions, and with all the difficulties that seemed to stand in the way, uniform law was pushed into the chimney corner of the Australian legal edifice, and there it long remained.

Early Attempts at Uniform Law

Only once before the late 1950's did it emerge for even a moment.[8] Following the adoption by Australia of the Paris Convention after World War I, the Commonwealth government had enacted regulations for the control of air navigation generally in Australia, as an exercise of its commerce power. In 1936, however, the High Court ruled that federal occupancy of the entire field of aviation—of intrastate as well as of interstate and international aviation—was unconstitutional without reference by the states under Section 51, subsection xxxvii, of the Commonwealth Constitution. The regulations

[7]*Proceedings of the Conference of Commonwealth and State Ministers* . . . *Canberra, July 7–8, 1952* (Canberra, 1952), p. 42.

[8] In 1921, the states, acting on their own, made an abortive attempt to deal by uniform law with an electoral matter—the right of members of a state parliament to become candidates for the Commonwealth Parliament without resigning their seats. A Commonwealth act settled the issue, however, before the states were able to act. See Gordon D. Combe, *Responsible Government in South Australia* (Adelaide, 1957), pp. 153–54, for a full discussion of the event.

were therefore null and void as they applied intrastate. By this time, Australia had learned the importance of aviation to the development and integration of its vast territories, and the Commonwealth immediately sought an amendment to the Constitution to allow federal control over the entire field of aviation. As might have been expected, the attempt failed. The Australian people were no more willing to change their Constitution for that purpose than for any other. Finally, in April 1937, the federal government convened a conference of Commonwealth and state ministers to discuss the problem. Prime Minister Menzies, who was then Attorney General of the Commonwealth, presided. There was immediate agreement as to the advantages of maintaining a single set of regulations for the entire country, and at Menzies' suggestion, the state representatives agreed to recommend to their parliaments enactment of uniform state acts that would simply adopt as state law the Commonwealth regulations on air navigation. Before the end of 1937, all six states had acted on the recommendations, and the "effect has been that, ever since, the regulations have applied uniformly to all classes of air navigation in Australia and their administration, whether as Federal or State law, has been vested in the Federal Authority."[9]

Although uniform legislation resulted from the discussions on aviation, it soon became obvious that no trend toward uniformity had been inaugurated. Uniform legislation in that case was demanded by a set of unusual and pressing circumstances. No one suggested that rules different from the federal regulations that had long been in force should be adopted. The states merely followed the dictates of logic and necessity in acting as they did. For a number of years thereafter, no advances were made in other fields at all.

The states did make one attempt to enact uniform law in 1942, when they sought to get together on a uniform income-

[9] *Australia in Facts and Figures,* No. 66, p. 87.

tax law. They differed so widely among themselves, however, as to "the severity of the taxation they imposed . . . the extent to which they relied on income taxes, and . . . the incidence of the tax"[10] that they were not able to get the project started. In the absence of state action, the Commonwealth stepped in and promptly preempted the field. Uniform law, it seemed, had its deficiencies. Back to the chimney corner it went, there to remain for another ten years. Nor was the attempt to make it work successful even then, although the issue certainly had public sentiment strongly behind it. In postwar Australia, as in postwar America, there was a great deal of concern among parents and school and church leaders especially, about children and teenagers, whose morals might be affected by comic books emphasizing sex, crime, cruelty, violence, and horror. Representatives of all the states except Western Australia met in Sydney in July 1952 to consider the matter. They decided that all the states ought to enact uniform laws punishing those who sold printed matter that would tend to "deprave or corrupt persons whose minds are open to immoral influences" or that gave undue emphasis to "matters of sex." Once again, however, uniformity was impossible to attain. As it turned out, in the words of an Australian observer, "the statutes which four states adopted in 1953-55 were substantially different from one another, except for a correspondence of two of them . . . ," and the plan came to nought.[11]

The Situation Changes

By the midfifties the situation had changed, even as Alfred Deakin had predicted it would, when he declared in 1903

[10] K. H. Bailey, "The Uniform Income Tax Plan (1942)," *Economic Record*, XX (1944), 171-72.

[11] Fitzpatrick, *Australian Commonwealth*, p. 50. Fitzpatrick gives the wording of the resolution adopted in Sydney. The four states were South Australia, Victoria, Queensland, and New South Wales.

that "Some day . . . the real unity of the six little streams of public affairs will become obvious as they are more and more brought together. Reciprocal relations will be fostered under the growing pressure of [common] ideals, needs, activities, and the mutual understandings begotten of mutual interests."[12] Although the Commonwealth had expanded its sphere of influence in Australian life throughout the depression and then the war, by the 1950's it was becoming increasingly obvious that it had about reached the limits of its power in a number of fields of activity under the Constitution. The High Court had not liberalized its interpretation of the Constitution, and the people were no more anxious to amend it than they had ever been. The Commonwealth thus was beginning to feel the need of some way to meet problems that it felt demanded a single solution but it was estopped by the Constitution from providing the solution itself. At the same time, the states, especially New South Wales and Victoria, began to seek a way to attack some of the same problems by positive state action. Both the states and the Commonwealth, particularly after Sir Garfield Barwick became Commonwealth Attorney General in 1958, came to the same conclusion: uniform law, despite its record, might be an answer to both their needs.

Hire Purchase

The first occasion to test that conclusion arose in the last months of 1957 in connection with the control of installment buying—hire purchase, as it is known in Australia.[13] Hire purchase was nothing new; it had been employed for years in buying cars. The increased availability of television sets after World War II, however, caused its use to burgeon. Both to

[12] Quoted in Davis (ed.), *Government of the Australian States*, p. 550.
[13] For a full discussion of hire purchase in Australia, see "Hire Purchase," *Current Affairs Bulletin*, XXIV, No. 1 (May 11, 1959).

purchase the sets themselves and to finance purchase of the products so tantalizingly advertised thereon, Australians in ever-growing numbers began to take advantage of hire purchase agreements. In every state, but again most keenly in New South Wales and Victoria, the rapid expansion of that credit device had both political and economic overtones, and some sort of regulation of its use was increasingly recognized as necessary. The matter was not within the competency of the Commonwealth government, as it lacks any power to intervene in intrastate commerce, and even when New South Wales asked the Commonwealth to convoke an interstate conference to discuss the problem, it declined both out of skepticism as to the result and by reason of its limited interest in the matter. New South Wales then took it upon herself to call a meeting of premiers and attorneys general of the states in Sydney in the summer of 1957-1958. The Commonwealth had a representative at the meeting, though not a person of ministerial rank, and throughout the discussion, he confined his role to that of an observer. There was unanimous agreement right away among the representatives of the states that some sort of controlling legislation was needed and that for its maximum effectiveness it should be uniform among the states. But they were far from agreement as to how to achieve that goal. Victoria, fortunately, had already gone so far by herself as to have a bill regulating hire purchase in her legislative mill, and for lack of an alternative proposal, the states agreed to work from it in developing a model bill. At first progress was slow, but gradually areas of agreement began to emerge, and after about twelve months (and after the decision to leave out the most difficult point—regulation of interest rates and deposits) a draft acceptable to all the states was secured. Victoria then substituted the model bill for the one she had originally prepared, and it was passed on May 12, 1959. Very shortly thereafter, the bill was introduced in and passed by all the other state parliaments and by the Commonwealth Parliament for the mainland territories.

The experience with the bill on hire purchase marked a turning point in the use of uniform law in Australia, not only because the bill was adopted but even more because attention was focused on uniform law. Important too was the fact that in the course of the meetings on hire purchase, a considerable degree of rapport developed among the state representatives. Certainly no one group of officers had ever sat together so long and worked in such depth before, and by the time they had completed their job, they felt a unity and an *esprit de corps* that was entirely new. At least to Arthur Rylah, attorney general and deputy premier of Victoria, and to several of the other state leaders involved, such an asset was too valuable to be allowed to deteriorate, especially when the country was faced with another problem to which uniform law, as they saw it, was a possible solution. The need was urgent just then for a more effective law regulating the formation and activities of private trading companies, and the group turned its very considerable talents to an attempt to channel its new accord in the direction of a uniform corporation code.

Company Law

At the time, Australian company law was badly in need of revision and updating. Although rooted in English example, it had long since begun to diverge from the original and to differ in each state from the law in force in the others. Some of the states had kept their acts for the most part up to date; others had not. By the midfifties, the New South Wales act had gone over twenty years without revision and Tasmania's, nearer fifty. In the meantime, the ramifications of modern commerce had become so widespread in Australia that they could no longer be adequately controlled by separate and divergent laws. Rapid communications, the increasing tendency of large industrial organizations to take over smaller ones, and the consequent concentration of capital in a small number of industrial giants all combined to make better regulation necessary. Moreover, experience under the existing acts showed that "many snide operators [had] been able to take advantage of the opportunities afforded them by the confusion and loopholes in the existing Companies Acts . . . in many instances to the disaster of the small investor."[14] There was no possibility that Commonwealth legislation could be devised to meet the need, for the High Court still maintained its 1909 position that the Constitution conferred no power on the Commonwealth to create corporations or to regulate their activities.[15] Four times—in 1911, 1913, 1919, and 1926—the Australian people had been asked to amend the Constitution so as to give that power to the Commonwealth, and four times they had turned the proposal down. The only recourse was thus to seek remedial action through state legislation.

Although the state premiers had agreed on the principle of uniform company law at the Premiers' Conference in 1946 and had reiterated their agreement at the Conference six years later,[16] the occasion for converting principle into practice did not arise until Victoria issued a call for a conference of attorneys general on the subject. The Commonwealth, as a result of an earlier decision of the Premiers' Conference, had already made some approaches to the states about uniform company law, and it gave its enthusiastic support to the project. Perhaps nothing would have happened even then had not company representatives themselves begun to see the

---

[14] *Parliamentary Debates, Legislative Assembly, Queensland, First Session of the 36th Parliament*, No. 23, 6 and 7 December, p. 2156.
[15] See Sawer, *Federalism in Australia*, pp. 5–6.
[16] *Proceedings of the Conference of Commonwealth and State Ministers*, p. 42.

need for revision and uniformity in the law under which they operated, and to make their wishes felt politically, and had not Sir Garfield Barwick, then Commonwealth attorney general, taken leadership in the matter. In any case, beginning in 1959 and continuing on through 1960, a series of meetings of state and Commonwealth ministers and departmental officers was held, at which the whole matter was raised for consideration. It was agreed at the outset to follow the lesson of hire purchase and use an existing act as the basis for discussion, this time the Victorian Company Act of 1958. Throughout the period, consultations were held with accountants and lawyers and with brokers and officers of chambers of commerce, as well as with leading industrial and financial figures in the Commonwealth. The meetings also had before them "the American Law Institute's Model Business Corporations Act . . . the existing company legislation of England and other Commonwealth countries . . . the evidence given so far to Lord Jenkins' Committee, which [then was] enquiring into certain suggestions for amendment to the British Act, and Professor Gower's proposals for Ghana."[17] Toward the end of 1960, a first draft was agreed upon and circulated, and comments were solicited from interested parties. The final draft, which took account of some of the suggestions received, was ready to be submitted to the seven parliaments in 1961. The end product was a work of monumental proportions—384 sections and 10 schedules, totalling altogether some 385 pages. It represents a major milestone in company administration in Australia.[18] By early 1963, the uniform bill had been passed by the parliaments of all the states and had been adopted by ordinance in the territories. It is now in effect throughout Australia.

[17] Sir Kenneth Bailey to author, May 2, 1962.
[18] For a concise summary of the contents of the law, see *Australia in Facts and Figures*, No. 74, pp. 109–10.

Standing Committee of Attorneys-General and Other Groups

So much progress within so short a length of time after so long a period of inactivity is phenomenal in itself, but still more important for the future of uniform law in Australia is the permanency that the machinery used to develop the hire purchase and company acts seems to have acquired. Neither the Commonwealth nor the states seem inclined to call a halt to the activities of the attorneys general now that those two acts have been launched. Having come together on a fairly regular basis for more than three years, the representatives of the seven governments have by now acquired an expertise that is unique in Australia. So well have they learned to work together, indeed, that both among themselves and in the press the group has accepted a Victorian suggestion to call itself the Standing Committee of the Attorneys-General of the Commonwealth and the States. Even without formal establishment under that name, it gives every indication of remaining active. The governments involved have accepted the role of the committee, and in recognition of that fact, again at Victorian suggestion, they have established regular administrative arrangements for staffing it. Each state has appointed a permanent liaison officer to the Standing Committee. These officers "collectively are not only channels of communication on the work of the Committee but form a kind of nucleus Working Party of Officers for consultation and planning. Collectively they constitute something very close to a diffuse and rudimentary, but so far an effective secretariat."[19] What is more, the committee's methods of procedure have become institutionalized to a surprising degree. At the meetings of the attorneys general, who in the Australian constitutional system are senior members of the cabinet, and as such, important mem-

[19] Sir Kenneth Bailey to author.

bers of the political executive of the states, the broad areas of possible action in the particular field of law under consideration are laid out, and the details are then referred to state experts at lower levels, who meet frequently and iron out differences in points of law between them. The liaison officers have established the habit of getting together before the Standing Committee meets, to prepare the agenda for it, and then again afterwards, to dispose of any details arising out of the committee's discussions. (For some while, when the company act was being prepared, the officers met every month or so, and the Standing Committee only a little less often.) The final product is then ready for reference back to the several state cabinets. Since the attorneys general, as members of those cabinets, have been acting in the committee's meetings with their cabinets' full knowledge and approval, the proposed legislation obviously has an excellent chance of adoption. Indeed, the key to the success of the uniform law movement to date can probably be found in the important fact that the legislation has been framed not only by experts in the law but by leaders of the parties in power in the states.

All the parties concerned in the evolution of the two uniform acts so far developed have attended meetings regularly and have been conscientious in performing their homework assignments. Some of the state officials admit that they are impelled to attend to these new duties not so much out of enthusiasm for them as because they want to be sure that the peculiar interests of their own states are not prejudiced or overlooked. And there is some indication that representatives of the younger states come because they want assurance that the discussions will not be unduly dominated by Victoria and New South Wales. Whatever their motive for attending, once they are together, they have found it easy to work with each other. The accomplishments of each meeting vary, of course, but the committee has discovered large areas of agreement, and as they are explored, it becomes steadily easier to move ahead to a harmonious decision. The operation of the committee has thus given Australia what it has never had before—a regularly constituted and peculiarly potent force, acting on state initiative, rather than on federal, working steadily for the adoption of uniform law. If the Standing Committee continues to develop as it now promises to and achieves other notable successes as it does so, perhaps the driving force for uniform law that has so far been lacking will have been supplied. If so, the creation of an Australian equivalent to the American and Canadian conferences may not be necessary.

Whatever its future, the Standing Committee is moving ahead on a number of fronts. It has already considered the existing state and Commonwealth laws governing the registration of business names, and a model bill reflecting the agreement reached on the subject has already been passed by all the states, although there is considerably more variation in the legislation adopted in the various states than in the case of the company law. The Standing Committee has also listed for consideration the following subjects:[20] amendment of uniform hire purchase act; uniform legislation on credit sales; uniform legislation covering money-lending and "fringe" banking operations; uniform service and execution of process acts; uniform legislation enabling the enforcement of fines interstate; uniform legislation providing for liens for subcontractors; uniform laws relating to the packaging of goods; uniform legislation controlling the sale of human blood; uniform acts dealing with spraying of chemicals from aircraft and on the ground (crop dusting); uniform laws covering the adoption of children; uniform acts relating to the maintenance of wives and children; uniform legislation providing for reciprocal enforcement of foreign civil judgments; extension by uniform law of the liability of air carriers for accidents in

20 *Ibid.*

intrastate flights; and uniform legislation for handling nuclear ships in Australian ports.

Whether because of the example of the Standing Committee and the interest shown by the states in the recommendations so far made by the committee, or because the logic of the ideas has finally been accepted, enthusiasm for uniform law has finally begun to spread to other groups in Australia as well. A draft for uniform poisons legislation was adopted by the National Health and Medical Research Council in 1959, and the Commonwealth Minister for Health has recently been urging its passage by the states. The Australian Advisory Transport Council has initiated discussion of a uniform road transport act and is in the process of drawing up a uniform traffic code.[21] The Sydney Water Board and the Melbourne Metropolitan Board of Works have been requested by the Conference of Water Supply and Sewerage Engineers to examine the possibility of developing uniform laws governing plumbing and drainage, and the Standards Association of Australia has been asked to set up a committee with representatives of the government and of private enterprise to draft an Australian standard for water and sewerage laws.[22] Such varied groups of state officials as those concerned with fighting bush fires, administering child welfare legislation, conserving fauna, and regulating weights and measures have also shown an interest in uniform law. It would almost appear that a boom in uniform law is belatedly getting underway in Australia.

Limited Appeal of Uniform Law

To date, however, the whole movement has been the product of government officials and chiefly those of the states. The Commonwealth has given hearty cooperation, but the

21 See *supra*, pp. 62-65.
22 E. L. Beers, Secretary, Metropolitan Water, Sewerage and Drainage Board, Sydney, to author, January 14, 1963.

direction of the movement has been largely determined by state officials. Enthusiasm for the idea does not seem to have spread very far beyond state interests. Although the Law Council of Australia has actively cooperated with the work of the Standing Committee, neither it nor other important legal and professional groups have as yet become ardent advocates of uniform law. A boom may not actually develop until they align themselves behind the movement. In part, the hesitation of other groups to endorse uniform law may reflect the opposition to its expanded use that was powerfully expressed in the 1959 *Report from the Joint Committee on Constitutional Review* to the Commonwealth Parliament. Over and over again, the committee pointed in its report to "the insurmountable difficulties" that would be encountered in trying to obtain "the approval of six independent States to a single course of action." "It would be much better from the public viewpoint," it went on, "if there were a single set of laws and regulations applied by one authority. . . . One set of technical experts could combine to have a knowledge and strength which several separate authorities could scarcely be expected to attain. Single legal control would ensure that uniform standards . . . were observed and would facilitate the task of amending legislation to take account of changing knowledge. . . . Sole responsibility should also make for uniformity in the enforcement of the provisions of the law. Lack of suitable legislation in only one State could seriously impair the control in other States."[23]

Although the subject under discussion then was nuclear energy, the committee reached the same conclusion for every other subject it considered. Even as to civil aviation, where uniform acts had been in effect for over twenty-five years, the committee noted that the "maintenance of the scheme of control depends . . . on the continued co-operation of the

[23] Commonwealth of Australia, *Report from the Joint Committee on Constitutional Review, 1959* (Canberra, 1959), pp. 80, 107.

states" and recommended a constitutional amendment to vest power over all aspects of aviation in the Commonwealth.[24] Indeed, the committee's recommendation in every case was an increase in Commonwealth power rather than an attempt to act by uniform legislation. As its conviction was so strong, it is doubtful whether the recent happy experiences with hire purchase and company law would have greatly modified the committee's stand, had it reported after those developments took place. Although there is no way of telling precisely how much concurrence with the committee's views exists in Australia today, they nevertheless represent the thinking of some of Australia's leading political figures[25] and thus must be assumed to be fairly widely held. If so, until they are altered, the further development of uniform law may well be frustrated.

Obstacles to Future Development

As proposals for uniform acts in each individual field are brought forward, opposition can always be expected, if only from those who have been benefitting from the lack of such legislation in the past. No sooner did it become known, for example, that the Standing Committee was discussing uniform laws against restrictive trade practices than the Australian business community raised flags of caution, the President of the Hobart (Tasmania) Chamber of Commerce warning solemnly that "commerce and industry must now make adequate preparation . . . for the closest examination of the proposed legislation. . . ."[26] In addition, opposition can be expected from time to time on party grounds. An attempt

[24] *Ibid.*, p. 69.
[25] The committee consisted of Senator Neil O'Sullivan, Chairman, Senators P. J. Kennelly, N. E. McKenna, Reg. C. Wright, and the following members of the House of Representatives: The Leader of the Opposition, Arthur A. Calwell, A. R. Downer, D. H. Drummond, Len. W. Hamilton, P. E. Joske, Reg. T. Pollard, E. J. Ward, and E. G. Whitlam.
[26] Hobart *Mercury*, October 21, 1961, p. 28.

on the part of Victoria to bring about uniformity between its workman's compensation law and that of New South Wales failed only in December 1962 through the pressures of party politics,[27] and the same thing can happen again on other issues. Opposition can also be expected from time to time from the so-called junior states of the Commonwealth against too much pressure for uniformity from New South Wales and Victoria. When the company bill was first proposed in South Australia, one of the leaders of the Opposition in the South Australian parliament at once asserted that "its provisions . . . could well place all South Australian businesses at the mercy of the bigger eastern States and overseas concerns"[28] and for that reason urged its defeat. Similar reactions may be forthcoming from Tasmania and Western Australia when the issue is one that rubs them the wrong way. Finally, some opposition may be forthcoming right along on account of the difficulties involved in getting uniform law adopted. Even though they can be overcome, as the hire purchase and company law instances make clear, they have been bruited about so much that they still have power to frighten the cautious.

Nor is the device of the Standing Committee a fully guaranteed one. It is composed of political personages, and the political situation in the several states varies a good deal. Not only are there party differences between the states, and between some of the states and the Commonwealth government, but because of the parliamentary system, elections come at different times, which may mean a changing membership on the Committee itself. Moreover, the whole enterprise is new enough so that no forms or procedures have yet been developed to handle the work that must be done on uniform law in the states. No state has personnel whose specific duties include consideration of proposals for uniform law. Apart from the committee, all work on the proposals

27 Melbourne *Age*, December 13, 1962, p. 1.
28 Adelaide *Advertiser*, October 16, 1961, p. 3.

thus must be accommodated, where and when it can, to busy state officials' regular—and to them probably more important—work. Without some better arrangement than this, one that would permit close and regular attention to the problems of working out mutually acceptable uniform acts, it is doubtful if the movement for uniform law will develop as quickly as it might. And there is a powerful anti-Commonwealth feeling in the states—a suspicion of Commonwealth motives, as it were—which must be taken into account. Should the Commonwealth come to assert too much leadership in bringing uniform law about—which it has not tried to do so far—it might work against the spread of uniform law. State political leaders are always wary lest their own parliaments become mere rubberstamps of Commonwealth-inspired legislation. The Commonwealth, everyone realizes, has greater and more specialized manpower resources that it could assign to work on uniform legislation, and the states would be reluctant to take what might come from Canberra without a careful analysis of each and every proposition. Given the intricate subject matter of many of the fields of uniform law, the danger that the Commonwealth might bring before them matters that they know little about or that are beyond their current needs and interests seems to be a real one to the states, however improbable it may be in actuality. In fact, to date, the Commonwealth has regarded the movement as primarily a state matter. Certainly, in many of the questions that the Standing Committee has listed on its agenda, the Commonwealth's interest is secondary, compared with that of the states. It is indicative of the Commonwealth's attitude that the Standing Committee has met in Canberra only once.

The Future of Uniform Law

Despite all these caveats against it, however, the conclusion is inevitable that uniform law, now that it has been tried, can hardly help growing in Australia. Three reasons support this assertion. First of all, uniform law supplies a way to clear the hurdles that the federal system imposes on government action, hurdles that have been getting increasingly irksome to both the Commonwealth and the states. Speaking of the traffic situation in Australia, for example, one of Australia's leading newspapers commented editorially in 1961 that there was "no reason why in a few years interstate hauliers and motorists touring beyond their own States should not be guided by rules which are very largely uniform. Easily understood laws should conduce to better driving and to the safe, smooth flow of traffic on the roads."[29] The fact that responsibility for the subject is divided among the states should not be regarded as justifiable reason to prevent the development of a uniform approach to the problems. The same kind of reasoning applies in the field of water conservation. State laws concerning the use of water are far from uniform. Queensland, for example, does not issue licenses for water use; New South Wales does. The difference in their practices creates problems, particularly in the management of the Great Artesian Basin, which lies under both states. Uniformity of practice would be a great help there. The advantages of uniform law can be demonstrated in field after field. Certainly one of the virtues of federalism is the room it allows for experiment, and perhaps no experiment promises such rich rewards as the further extension of uniform law.

Secondly, the process for developing uniform law as it has been worked out since 1957 in Australia has much to recommend it. It assures that the best thinking in the country, as well as the most pertinent examples from overseas, will be brought to bear on every problem being considered, thus providing an expertise in drafting legislation that has heretofore been lacking in most of the states. No one of the state parliaments nor that of the Commonwealth is under any

29 *Ibid.*, October 25, 1961, p. 2.

compulsion to adopt a recommended act, so that in order to pass, a proposal must have intrinsic merit.

Finally, uniform law suggests itself as a method of limiting Commonwealth power, a method that the states can bring to bear whenever the time is right. Nor are the states unaware of this possibility. Thus in April 1962 Premier Bolte of Victoria remarked that the "states are now waking up to the dangers of centralized government from Canberra." "This is one reason," the premier concluded, "why the States got together on uniform company law, and other matters."[30] The implications of Premier Bolte's remarks are obvious. The public has already invested the Standing Committee with the status of an all-state movement, and as the Australian states seek to use their own powers in a positive way to check the expansion of Commonwealth power at their expense, they will find, even as did the American states before them, that interstate cooperation is a powerful bow, for which uniform law serves as a sound and reliable arrow.

The future of uniform law in Australia is still uncertain. An impressive beginning has been made in hire purchase and company law, and there is some activity in a number of other areas. There is, however, no widespread excitement about the idea as yet throughout the Commonwealth. If it has active partisans, it also has powerful opponents, and probably the bulk of the Australian people are indifferent to the whole movement. Even the attitude of the Commonwealth government toward uniform law can hardly be regarded as fixed. With a different attorney general in office, or with a different political party in power, the uniform law movement could easily be sidetracked. One does not have to be a very serious student of public administration to recognize that governmental interest comes and goes. Even if its interest remains keen, the Commonwealth will probably move slowly. Too much pressure might be worse than too little.

[30] Melbourne *Age*, April 6, 1962, p. 6.

In the last analysis, however, the factors which will determine the future of uniform law will be the specific needs of the growing Australian nation. In the areas of commercial and family law in particular, as well as in certain areas of legal procedure, state lines in Australia are already coming to have less and less meaning. As the Commonwealth becomes one interdependent social and economic unit, it must rely increasingly on common action by the states. The use of uniform law in such action has been successfully tested, and in the years ahead, it may well come to be a major factor in Australian federalism.

Chapter 7

THE FUTURE OF
INTERSTATE RELATIONS

The explicit prediction that interstate relations will be further
developed in Australia seems fully warranted. The benefits
that state cooperation have brought seem enough alone to
guarantee its continued—and expanded—use in the future.
A better guarantee still is the large number of problems that
await solution in a country as young as Australia. In attacking
a great many of them, interstate cooperation can be a useful
weapon. It would not be possible to list all the problems of
development facing Australia, and it would be foolish to
attempt to assign priorities for solving those that have been
identified. But some suggestions for interstate action nevertheless are feasible.

Regional Development

Opportunities for interstate cooperation exist in the development of the Riverina, the rich Murray Valley area west
from Albury to Swan Hill and beyond, which lies on the
border between New South Wales and Victoria. The diversion of the Snowy's waters will vastly add to the agricultural
potential of the whole area, and in developing this area,
cooperation between the two states would be productive in
such matters as policies for land settlement, conservation
and irrigation, control of crop diseases and floods, schemes for
marketing new products, transportation and communication
facilities, and research and planning generally. The same kind
of joint effort toward regional development might also be

made in the coastal resort area running from Southport in Queensland to Tweed Heads in New South Wales.

Another possibility is the management and development of the forests that cover much of the land along the New South Wales-Victoria border. These states already cooperate in fighting forest fires, but the possibilities are much broader than that. To be effective, work to eradicate insects, disease, and blight ought to be undertaken on an interstate basis. Cooperation on research into soil deficiencies and drainage problems makes equally good sense. And attention might be given to the possibility of rescuing the submerged red-gum forests on both sides of the Murray River through some kind of cooperative effort. The River Murray Commission itself might undertake that task. In the next decade or so, demands for wood can be expected to mount rapidly in Australia, and forest improvement through combined efforts of the states can be a great help in meeting them.

Higher Education

Another area for possible joint action by the states is the development of higher education in Australia. All the universities in Australia, with the exception of Canberra University College and the Australian National University, are state universities—not quite in the American sense of the term, but at least the creatures of a state charter, state supported, and with state representation on their governing boards. Through the years, each university has largely pursued its own independent way,[1] and in simpler days, when a university's chief function, in Australia as elsewhere, was regarded as being chiefly concerned with the undergraduate education of a few, this independence was not a liability. But by the 1960's, a quite different concept of the university's

[1] Percy H. Partridge, "The Australian Universities and Governments," *Australian Teacher*, XXXVII (January 1960), 31.

role had developed. Not only had numbers become a problem, but the demands of a changing society had forced universities to place heavy emphasis on graduate instruction and research, the most expensive aspects of university operation—and none of the states is wealthy enough to carry on a full program in both areas by itself. Although the Commonwealth has recently altered the picture both by providing a good deal of financial support and by establishing the Australian National University as a graduate and research university, the state universities still continue to bear the major burden for the development of these aspects of higher education in Australia. As they plan for the future, the actions of American state universities provide a model they might well follow. The southern states were faced with a problem very similar to Australia's after World War II, and their answer was to join forces by means of an interstate compact to provide for joint planning and use of university resources so as to avoid costly duplication and competition for staff, facilities, and programs in graduate and professional areas. The Southern Regional Education Board, which administers the compact, now embraces sixteen states, and since its creation in 1949 it has had an outstanding record of success.[2] The southern pattern was followed in New England and the West,[3] and both those areas are obtaining impressive results from their joint programs. For the Australian states to follow the same general line of action would not be difficult. Already there are signs that thinking is running in that direction. Should not the universities, asks Professor Partridge, "try to evolve . . . policies of future expansion . . . which will . . . provide for some measure of specialization in the different

[2] Redding S. Sugg, Jr., and George Hilton Jones, *The Southern Regional Education Board* (Baton Rouge, 1960) provides a well-written account of the origins, development, and present status of the board and its programs.
[3] The New England Board of Higher Education and the Western Interstate Commission on Higher Education are the respective administrative agencies of the two education compacts in those regions.

universities, for the encouragement of particular sorts of studies in particular places?"[4] How better—how else, for that matter—could this be done than by some form of interuniversity cooperation? The Committee on Australian Universities made some specific suggestions to this end in its 1957 report,[5] and the Australian Universities Commission, which was created at the committee's suggestion two years later, will no doubt make other recommendations, for the act that established the commission requires it to "perform its functions with a view to promoting the balanced development of universities so that their resources can be used to the greatest possible advantage of Australia."[6] In addition, Prime Minister Menzies appointed a special Committee on the Future of Tertiary Education in 1962, and when it has completed its study, the chances are it too may recommend cooperation.

Leadership toward interstate cooperation in higher education may also be expected from the vice chancellors, who have already formed the habit of meeting together regularly to discuss university affairs. No one in the Australian university world knows its needs and problems better than they do. University registrars and accountants also meet together regularly, and they too are fully cognizant of institutional needs. Any or all of these groups might begin to explore the possibilities of joint action on higher education. There is no reason to believe the method would work any less well in Australia than it has in the United States.

Bush Fire Fighting

Although the four eastern states have already learned the value of cooperation in fighting bush fires, there is still a great

4 Partridge, "Australian Universities and Governments," p. 32.
5 Commonwealth of Australia, *Report of the Committee on Australian Universities* (Canberra, 1957); see also "The Murray Report on Australian Universities," *Current Affairs Bulletin*, XXI, (March 24, 1958).
6 Commonwealth of Australia, *An Act to Establish an Australian Universities Commission*, No. 30 of 1959, 14, (1).

deal that could be done jointly. From early October to late March every year, Australia lives in dread of the devastation caused by bush fires, and fires are no respecters of state boundaries. Thus in New South Wales the worst danger area is in the North Coast and Central North country, where the summer wind comes off the "hot plate" formed by the "parched, dry plains of South-western Queensland."[7] The southeastern boundary of New South Wales and Victoria and the long dry border between Victoria and South Australia are equally troublesome fire areas. Yet up to now, fire fighting has largely ignored the interstate nature of the fires themselves and has been organized on a state-by-state basis. As the years have gone by, modern equipment and facilities have made this organizational pattern increasingly obsolete. The most important weapons in fighting bush fires today are the helicopter and the aerial tanker.[8] Both items, however, are very expensive. In 1961, the Forestry Commission of New South Wales, which had only about £ 300,000 to spend on firefighting altogether, did not have sufficient funds even to hire a helicopter, much less buy one, and this in the face of testimony by a veteran firefighter that if New South Wales "dries out into a real tinder box, to have a couple of 'choppers' on patrol could mean the difference between beating a fire . . . or having millions of acres burnt black."[9] Obviously, the necessary equipment might be bought, if there were interstate arrangements for sharing the costs of buying and maintaining it. Two or three separate ones might be made, one between New South Wales and Victoria, another between New South Wales and Queensland, and perhaps a third between Victoria and South Australia. In addition, an Interstate Bush Fire Protection Commission, perhaps modeled after the Northeastern Interstate Forest Fire

---

[7] David Burke, "A Black Summer Menaces the Bush," Sydney Sun-Herald, October 8, 1961, p. 25.

[8] See R. H. Luke, Bushfire Control in Australia (London, 1961).

[9] Quoted by Burke, "A Black Summer."

Protection Commission in the United States, might be formed by all four states to administer the agreements and to serve as a planning and coordinating body for them all.

Underground Water Resources

Still another opportunity for interstate cooperation exists in the use and control of Australia's underground water resources. Four of the five largest artesian basins in Australia are interstate. The Great Artesian Basin—the largest known artesian basin in the world—covers some 670,000 square miles under Queensland, New South Wales, South Australia, and the Northern Territory. Over three thousand bores have been put down in the basin, and water from them sustains a large pastoral industry in the area. The other basins have not been exploited to quite such an extent, but the possibilities of their use are exciting. The Murray Basin covers some 107,000 square miles under Victoria, New South Wales, and South Australia; the Eucla Basin, 68,000 square miles under Western Australia and South Australia; the Barkly Basin, another 57,000 square miles under Queensland and the Northern Territory; and the Ord–Victoria Region Basin, a still undetermined amount of territory under northern Western Australia and the Northern Territory. Altogether, these basins supply water for "at least 20 per cent of the sheep and a large number of the cattle in Australia."[10] Although much of the water from these basins is presently saline and suitable only for stock, some of it is high quality, quite usable for domestic and industrial purposes. All of it, however, constitutes a valuable natural resource in so arid a country as Australia. The cooperative pattern set by the River Murray Commission for the allocation and control of the chief surface waters in the Commonwealth has not been followed, however, in dealing with underground water. There is a great deal of

[10] *Australia in Facts and Figures*, No. 62 (June quarter 1959), p. 41.

variation among state laws on the subject, and considerable waste and careless and inefficient use of water takes place as a result. At first, the nature of the artesian process was poorly understood, but intense scientific effort has demonstrated that diminution of flow is the most serious problem in all the basins.[11] Cooperation among the states is obviously vital if the problem is to be attacked with any success. Although some progress has been made in other aspects of the underground water problem—the adoption of uniform methods of recording data and the conduct of joint research programs into artesian water problems, for example—and more will undoubtedly be forthcoming when the newly created Australian Water Resources Council becomes operative, no progress has been made so far in regulating and controlling the use of this water. The governments concerned have been prodded and warned, but as yet they have not taken any steps to remedy the situation.[12] The direction of their steps is clear. They can lead nowhere but to interstate cooperation.

Rail Standardization

The mainland states must finally act together in the matter of rail standardization.[13] Despite the improvements in service in recent years, what Sir Harold Clapp said in 1946 is still too true: "[The] diversity of [railway] gauges makes Australia's railway system a loose combination of independent units and contributes greatly to State parochialism. It divides Australia virtually into 'five islands' instead of welding us into one great

---

11 *Ibid.*

12 See the call for action by W. H. R. Nimmo, President of the Institution of Engineers, Australia, reprinted under the title, "The World's Water Supply and Australia's Portion of It," *Journal of the Institution of Engineers, Australia*, XXI (March 1949), 1–6.

13 See Eric Harding, *Uniform Railway Gauge* (Melbourne, 1958), for a detailed account of the problem and the progress made in solving it. Mr. Harding was formerly Secretary of Commonwealth Railways. See also N. McCusker, "Standard Gauge Railways System," *Public Administration*, XXI (March 1962), 15–20.

nation."[14] And more than that. Railway operating costs are too high in Australia as a result of breaks in gage, and inefficiency, delay, and damage in transshipment are still all too common. There is little doubt that failure to standardize will continue to be a boon to bus and truck transport in the Commonwealth, as it has in the past, perhaps diverting as much as 500,000 tons of traffic a year.[15] But even if the need is great, every state line need not be converted to standard gage. Conversion could be confined to main lines, and it need not take place all at once. As old tracks and equipment wear out, replacements could be made in standard gage. Whatever is done, however, must be done jointly by the several state systems. Cooperation in the matter, indeed, may be the only way in the long run to prevent the Commonwealth from stepping in and taking over the railways for the sake of Australia's economic future.[16]

Preservation of Kangaroos

Even on a number of minor matters, there is ample room for interstate cooperation—regulating the killing of kangaroos, for example. An estimated one million kangaroos are slaughtered every year, and if this rate is continued, the distinctive Australian marsupial will soon be as near extinction as the remarkable American buffalo, to everyone's loss and sorrow. The states now have varying game and health laws, so that there is no single policy for either the conditions for killing kangaroos or the sale of kangaroo meat throughout the country. By the enactment and enforcement of uniform laws on those subjects, the states could eliminate unnecessary slaughter.

[14] Clapp, "Australia—A Nation," p. 148.
[15] The estimate given in *Australia in Facts and Figures*, No. 59 (September quarter 1958), p. 101.
[16] See on this point the remarks of M. M. Bayne, "Transport in Victoria," in Leeper (ed.), *Introducing Victoria*, p. 149.

Cooperation in Law Enforcement

Or take the handling of interstate traffic cases. Until World War II there was not enough interstate automobile traffic in Australia for the occasional offender from out of state to cause much concern anywhere. Today, Australians roam all over their continent by car, and in the process Victorians break Queensland road laws, Queenslanders break those in Western Australia, and so on down the list. In the fall of 1961, Queensland alone had four hundred warrants to be served on New South Wales and Victoria residents and 200 more for South Australians.[17] Yet no device now exists for easy reciprocity among the states in handling them. In fact, the states seem to be barred from working out a satisfactory cooperative arrangement by Commonwealth legislation covering the enforcement of court orders against traffic offenders in other states. That legislation needs to be amended, and the states need to find an agreeable joint solution.

Opportunities for Action

Indeed, the possibilities for the application of the device of interstate cooperation are far more numerous than these few suggestions would seem to indicate. In virtually every field of state governmental activity, there is some unexploited opportunity for interstate action. Interstate cooperation has by now been used extensively enough so that there is a considerable body of experience from which to draw, and this should be of great help to the founders of new interstate activities. Of help too would be a drive to secure an increased public awareness and appreciation of the potentialities of interstate cooperation. If that is achieved, the next few years may see interstate cooperation greatly extended in Australia.

17 Melbourne *Age*, October 24, 1961, p. 2.

Just how far interstate cooperation will be carried is hard to say. It is not necessarily true that merely bringing state officials together will automatically produce cooperation between them. T. H. Kewley has pointed out that although government statisticians from the states had been discussing the meaning of the term "governmental body" at their meetings for several years, they were unable to reach an "agreement upon a suitable definition, or definitions."[18] The same thing has happened and will continue to happen in other areas of concern. Australians, perhaps to a greater degree than other people, will never see eye to eye with each other on everything. Certainly, complete cooperation between the Australian states is impossible. The states are at least semisovereign, and even if they had the maximum desire to cooperate, their interests are not identical. Geography alone limits the number and kind of cooperative arrangements that can be worked out. But it is not important that complete cooperation exist in any case. What is important is that political and administrative officers of state governments recognize the advantages of interstate cooperation and that they are willing to use it when it is feasible to do so.

Nor can the future development of interstate cooperation be expected to be uniform among the states. The needs and problems of the states vary, and so do their traditional relations with one another. New South Wales and Victoria will no doubt continue for many years to house the bulk of the nation's population, industry, trade, and commerce and thus will face problems quite different than those encountered in Western Australia and to some extent in Queensland. Tasmania will continue for her part to encounter problems peculiar to an island. And South Australia can be expected to go on along her independent path in the future, as she has in

[18] T. H. Kewley, "The Statutory Corporation," in Spann (ed.), *Public Administration in Australia*, p. 109.

the past. The degree to which each state resorts to interstate cooperation will thus vary accordingly.

Need for Leadership

Without leadership, none of the states can be expected to turn to interstate cooperation much more than they have in the past. Although an increasing number of Australian state officials are aware of the availability of cooperative devices and of their advantages as well, a good many still are not. Unfortunately, this is more true of party leaders than of administrative personnel. Australian state politics, like those in the United States, are internally oriented. Political rewards are not won by achieving cooperation with other states, but by fighting and winning the political battle with local adversaries on local issues. The Deputy Leader of the Opposition in Western Australia is typical of many Australian political leaders in his reaction to the suggested use of interstate cooperation. He was sure as late as 1960 that "Interstate activities are virtually non-existent as far as governments are concerned. The separate States carry out their programmes without reference to other States. . . . [T]here is an interchange of information but that is as far as they go."[19] To the extent that such a belief continues to be held, the possibilities of extending the use of interstate cooperation are not very bright. Even among administrators—especially those below the top level in state departments—there is considerable indifference and ignorance as to the utility of interstate cooperation. Before the war and even since, a large proportion of the people recruited to the state public service have been school leavers only, not university graduates. They enter the service at about sixteen years of age, and if they get a university degree at all, it is apt to be much later and as a result of

[19] John Tomkin to author, March 22, 1960.

night school.[20] Whether the lack of higher education is to blame or a combination of causes, state public officials have been on the whole unimaginative, pedestrian, and parochial. Department officials often do not even think of coordinating their activities with those of fellow officials in other departments in their own states, to say nothing of thinking about coordination across state lines. The average senior public servant, S. R. Davis concludes in his study of state governments, earns his promotions "by patience in the queue, by diligence, reliability, and length of service rather than brilliance in innovating and executing imaginative policy measures; he will hold inflexibly to the convictions of his own administrative experiences and have little patience with novelties. . . ."[21] Certainly one of the reasons Commonwealth-state cooperation is so much further advanced than interstate relations is the higher caliber of Commonwealth public servants.

The picture is not all black, of course. The very existence of a thriving plant of interstate cooperation is proof that it is not. In every state, there are outstanding public servants, many of whom have been the leaders in the development of presently functioning schemes of joint action. But all state public services in Australia today "complain . . . of a tendency among young people 'to disregard the State . . . services when choosing a career,' and [of] the decline of efficiency in some branches . . . where the load of work has fallen on too few able shoulders. . . . This very problem, how to attract enough talent to their employ, is without doubt the most urgent and important single problem confronting the States

<hr>

[20] See for a general overview of the state public service B. B. Schaffer and K. W. Knight, *Top Public Servants in Two States* (Brisbane, 1963).

[21] Davis (ed.), *Government of the Australian States*, p. 699; his full discussion of this point (pp. 696–701) is well worth reading. Barbara Ward echoes Davis' conclusion. Australia is "a country of brilliant individual performance and relatively mediocre collective service or action," she remarked in "Clouds over the Australian Sun," *New York Times Magazine*, November 4, 1962, p. 104. See also on this point Hancock, *Australia*, p. 142, and Shaw, *Story of Australia*, pp. 274, 288.

today. . . . Their need is a dramatic show of boldness and imagination. Their failure to rise to the occasion will affect so much else because the States still bear the primary responsibility for developing important sectors of the public estate."[22] Nowhere is the need and the challenge posed by this problem more critical to future development than in the case of interstate cooperation.

Suggestions for the Future

It may be that, despite the development of the Premiers' Conference and a number of other high-level, permanent groups of state political leaders and officials, and more recently of the Standing Committee of Attorneys-General, the most effective kind of leadership will not be forthcoming until an organization dedicated specifically to the cause of interstate cooperation is established in Australia. At least it is a fair conclusion that in the United States, the widespread application of the techniques of interstate action results from the Council of State Governments and its agents in the states, the Commissions on Interstate Cooperation, aided and abetted in their work by the National Conference of Commissioners on Uniform State Laws. These groups keep the possibilities of cooperation in programs and in law constantly before the states and particularly before the state legislatures. And in Canada the Conference on Uniformity of State Legislation performs some of the same functions. Through their meetings, the research performed under their aegis, and the publicity they give to the idea of cooperation, an ever-growing number of state officials are acquainted with the possibilities in the field and encouraged to explore them. No such regular force exists for the propagation of the faith in Australia, and as a result, progress has been much slower. There are still areas in Australian state government where

[22] Davis (ed.), *Government of the Australian States*, p. 701.

cooperation as a concept has yet to be advanced for the first time. Until it is, and until it is allowed some time to be assimilated, it is fruitless to expect interstate cooperation to develop.

A body such as the American Council of State Governments should not be the only source of inspiration, however. An equally important contribution to the further use of interstate cooperation might be made by assigning the responsibility for collecting and disseminating information about cooperative possibilities among the units of state government to a specific officer in each state, who would perhaps also serve as its sponsor. The Premier's Department in several states has begun to exercise some of that function, but without any very clear assignment of responsibility to do so. That department is the logical one to serve as a channel of communication, but it could better perform the task if it were given to one particular person. Perhaps an interstate commissioner, such as has been used by some of the western states in the United States in the development of water distribution compacts, might be employed. Some sort of legislative arrangement to facilitate the passage of legislation might eventually need to be set up if interstate cooperation is really to be pushed in Australia. The American states provide a model of sorts in their Commissions on Interstate Cooperation, but as many of these are moribund, the Australian versions should be patterned only after the best American arrangements.[23]

To a large extent, the further advance of interstate cooperation in the Australian federal system depends on the support it receives from the Australian political parties. The Liberal and Country parties either have been the sponsors of or have supported most of the formalized interstate arrangements that have so far been developed in Australia. A reversal of their receptive attitude toward the device need not be antici-

[23]See Frederick L. Zimmermann and Richard H. Leach, "The Commissions on Interstate Cooperation," *State Government*, XXX (Autumn 1960), 233–42.

pated. The attitude of the Australian Labour Party towards its use is the critical question. From its beginning, the Labour Party has been committed to the eventual abolition of the states themselves and thus could never be an advocate of interstate cooperation. It has been consistent in its preference for Commonwealth action over state action every time and in either overlooking altogether or being severely critical of interstate cooperation and uniform state laws. Thus for example it reaffirmed at its 1961 Conference the decision it reached in 1957 that "for the purpose of co-ordinating transport in Australia a Federal body [should] be set up . . . with power to . . . control all types of interstate transport . . . [and] to fix rates and charges."[24] In recent years, however, because of the opposition of a number of state units of the party to the idea, the ALP has been less vocal about centralization and seems to have become more interested in interstate cooperation. The 1961 Conference even went so far as to approve formally of state attempts "to achieve uniform legislation for the operation and control of hire purchase businesses" (although it still could not resist noting elsewhere that federal legislation to control hire purchase would eventually be necessary "in view of the impossibility of obtaining general effective action by the various States").[25] And although it still recommends a Commonwealth authority in place of a state body whenever it can, as it did in recommending an Australian Conservation Authority to take the place of state activities in the field of water conservation,[26] it did make a concession in the field of education. The 1961 Conference decided: "That, in view of the increase in interstate migration, State Education Departments . . . [should] consider the desirability

[24] Australian Labour Party, *Official Report of the Proceedings of the 24th Commonwealth Conference* (1961), p. 45. See also its recommendations with regard to marketing of primary products and to mental health (pp. 42, 22).
[25] *Ibid.*, pp. 25, 28.
[26] *Australian Labour Party Policy for 1961 Election, National Development* (mimeographed release), p. 3.

and practicability of introducing some measure of uniformity
in the various State Education systems by annual coordination
of the States on matters of common interest . . . [such as] (i)
school commencing age, (ii) stages of transfer from primary
to secondary school, (iii) school leaving age, (iv) content in
basic subjects, (v) matriculation requirements."[27] Although
the recommendation was spoiled somewhat by an accompany-
ing one—that a federal Ministry of Education and Science be
created—it does suggest that the party's attitude toward the
utility and desirability of interstate cooperation may be undergoing a change. That conclusion is supported by a general
shift in tone in recent conference discussions in other areas.
If there is substance to such a shift, it could have an important
effect on the future development of interstate cooperation.

Whatever party or coalition is in power, the Australian
people will probably continue to be committed to the federal
system, to the coexistence of the state and the Commonwealth
governments. If so, in the long run they can hardly help
seeing the advantages of interstate cooperation both as a
device to strengthen state programs and as a bulwark against
expansion into state fields by the Commonwealth. At least
in the United States, there is no doubt that the postwar spurt
in interstate cooperative activities was due at least in part to
the determination by the states to do their jobs so well that
there would be no justification for the federal government to
step in and take over state functions. To date, the Australian
states have not seemed to want to avoid Commonwealth
intervention. Indeed, in some areas they have actively sought
it.[28] Thus so far the states have shown little evidence of

[27] Decision A. L. P. Federal Conference 1961, Education (mimeographed
release), "c".

[28] In several areas, the American states have also turned to the central
government for aid; highways, airport construction, and water-pollution control are outstanding examples. They have done so, however, for the most
part with outward reluctance and many protestations of dismay at having
to do so. The Australian states have been much more straightforward in
asserting the desirability of Commonwealth assistance.

cooperating from a desire to thwart the Commonwealth. Should the trend toward the expansion of Commonwealth powers be accelerated, however, as it might with the accession to power of the ALP, the states might well make greater use of interstate action in an attempt to slow the Commonwealth down or to stop it altogether.

But interstate cooperation need not be entered into negatively, merely as a last resort to stop the Commonwealth from extending too far its area of influence. It can and should be entered into positively, as a legitimate and sensible way of exercising state powers. The states naturally wish to preserve their own spheres of power, but at the same time it is important that they expand their range of services and activities to meet the demands of a developing nation. Interstate cooperation is one tool they can use with effect to that end.

All through this study, I have assumed that interstate cooperation is a good thing for Australia, and it probably is. In fact, however, too little is known about it now to permit a final judgment to be made. Interstate arrangements are still new, still developing. Moreover, too little attention has been paid to the whole matter for any firm conclusion to be drawn. Before final evaluation is made, the techniques of political science and public administration need to be used in a series of case studies in the major areas of interstate cooperation. In particular, studies of the impact of interstate cooperation on the political processes of the states, on the working of the federal system, and on the Commonwealth government need to be made. In the meantime, state political and administrative leaders will go right on conceiving new uses of interstate cooperation. Although it is too early to tell yet, it is not impossible that when analytical studies are finally made, they will demonstrate that interstate cooperation has become in Australia, as it has in the United States and Canada, a powerful instrument of government and a vital part of the machinery of Australian politics.

BIBLIOGRAPHICAL COMMENT

The footnotes to the foregoing chapters constitute a bibliography of sorts by themselves, and those citations are not repeated here. A number of comments about sources are in order, however.

First of all, although I have cited a number of works—and indeed would have been lost without them—the literature on Australian government and politics in general is still far from plentiful. Much of what does exist is descriptive, written for the general reader rather than for the serious student. The best works have been written by historians, not by political scientists or public administrators. A great many more entries, a good proportion of them analytical, are needed on the list before a thorough understanding of the Australian governmental system can be obtained. A good compilation of what does exist is contained in the bibliography prepared by A. G. L. Shaw for his *The Story of Australia,* which is cited above. It provides a good starting point for anyone interested either in Australia in general or in Australian government and federalism in particular. The problem of sources is much more difficult in the field of state government, and this is of immediate concern to the student of interstate relations. Alan Davies concluded in 1955 that state politics and administration were simply not very interesting to the average Australian (Davies, in Leeper, *Introducing Victoria,* p. 286), and this seems to have been equally true of the Australian scholar. Only S. R. Davis' book, which a glance at the footnotes reveals I used extensively, presents evidence to the contrary.

Secondly, as I pointed out several places in the text, the

whole subject of interstate relations has been neglected in
Australian research and writing on government and politics.
I know this to be the case not only because I searched in
vain for titles in every state and university library in Australia
and talked to scores of state officials about possible items I
might have missed, but also because each of the state librarians
in Australia conducted a literature search for me, and with
the exceptions I have noted, their findings were all the same:
there is simply no literature in the field. There are thus no
sources to list that pertain directly to my subject. Furthermore, it is even difficult to keep track of developments in the
field, except by word of mouth or through an occasional
newspaper story, so little attention is paid to interstate relations. Only the quarterly publication of the Australian News
and Information Bureau, on which I relied so heavily,
Australia in Facts and Figures, and the annual volume prepared by the Commonwealth Bureau of Census and Statistics,
Year Book of the Commonwealth of Australia, have anything
like full coverage of intergovernmental relations, and thus
incidentally of interstate relations. Their editors are evidently
some of the few people in Australia who understand the field
and are curious about its growth and development. The
several state yearbooks are considerably less perceptive, although an occasional reference to interstate arrangements is
to be found therein.

One or two other government publications are helpful.
The Queensland Government Public Relations Bureau quite
regularly puts out a *News Bulletin,* which sometimes contains
stories dealing with Queensland's relations with her sister
states. The Commonwealth Department of Health publishes a
monthly magazine, *Health,* which often refers to some interstate arrangement in its field, and the Commonwealth Director of Fisheries puts out a monthly *Fisheries Newsletter*
which helps one keep *au courant* with interstate activities in
that area.

None of the lay journals pay much attention to interstate

relations. *Public Administration*, the journal of the Australian Regional Groups of the Royal Institute of Public Administration, the *Australian Journal of Politics and History*, and *Historical Studies, Australia and New Zealand* carry articles bearing on the subject once in a while, as more rarely do such popular magazines as *Hemisphere* and the *Bulletin*. The April 1963 issue of *Hemisphere* (VII, 33-36), for example, contained an excellent little article by R. H. Reid on "Some Aspects of Political Thought in Australia," which dealt in part with the problem of federalism. Articles in all these journals, and in the few others that are published in Australia, are listed in the bulletins of the *Australian Public Affairs Information Service*, which are published monthly by the Commonwealth National Library in Canberra. Any serious student of interstate relations, as of any other area of Australian government, will want to make early and frequent use of the Service's bulletins.

The serious student would also want to tap the resources of the several Commonwealth and state governments themselves. Both the Commonwealth and the state parliaments and many of the departments of both governments publish reports that are valuable as far as interstate relations are concerned. Departmental annual or biennial reports are especially helpful. The footnotes to the chapters above mention the ones I found to be most significant. Merely dropping an air letter to the secretary of the particular department or departments one is interested in, asking to be placed on the mailing list for all regular and special reports, is enough to assure receiving them. Government departments are usually willing also to send copies of press releases upon request, and a number of these proved very useful to me. Printed government reports are generally indexed in the *Votes and Proceedings* of the Commonwealth and state parliaments, and careful study of those indexes is a necessary step in beginning a research project.

Unfortunately, few of the interstate bodies themselves do

very extensive reporting, the River Murray Commission and the Snowy Mountains Council constituting about the only exceptions. No records at all are kept of meetings of several of the most important interstate bodies—or if they are kept, they are circulated only within the group and are not made available for distribution. Often no report of the discussion in their meetings is even made to the press (hence the paucity of newspaper stories about interstate meetings). Thus no record is kept of the proceedings of the Loan Council or of the Australian Agricultural Council. The newly created Australian Fisheries Council established the same rule at its first meeting. Several others, including the prestigious Australian Port Authorities Association, follow the same practice. The theory of course is that keeping no verbatim minutes (and having no observers) fosters free and full discussion; however valid the theory, the practice is hard on the student of interstate relations.

In addition, several of the more formally organized conferences carry on publishing programs and are quite happy to add names to the mailing list for their reports. *Roads in Australia*, the yearly publication of the Conference of State Road Authorities, is an excellent example of this sort of thing. The political parties also publish occasional reports and brochures, and they are sometimes helpful to the student.

So the student is not totally without resources. Most of them are available readily, however, only in Australia. Few American libraries have much of what I have described here. Thus in the last analysis, nothing takes the place of the personal visit to Australia. Without innumerable personal interviews and frequent access to departmental files, studies of interstate relations of much depth are not possible.

Although I have commented a number of times on how little attention has so far been paid to interstate relations by Australian and other scholars, the situation is gradually improving. Besides the recently published works I have already cited, Bernard Schaffer of the University of Queensland has begun a study of state government in that state, and R. H. Reid of the University of Adelaide has a work in progress on South Australia. Both, I hope, will deal to some extent at least with interstate relations. There may be one or two others I have not heard about. In addition to work by mature scholars, there is some evidence that Australian and American professors of history and political science are beginning to guide their doctoral candidates toward the field of interstate cooperation. At least, David H. Provost completed a dissertation on federal-state cooperation in Australia at the University of Queensland in 1957, and John Merritt, of the same university, began one on the Premiers' Conference. And in the United States F. Burke Sheeran did a doctoral dissertation on Australian federalism for the University of Southern California in 1956, part of which was published under the title cited above in Chapter 5. Certainly there is room enough for a great many more dissertations on aspects of interstate relations in the years ahead.

Perhaps the most helpful thing that could happen would be the establishment of the field as a recognized subarea of intergovernmental relations in general, so that indexers and bibliographers in Australia would catch pertinent items more readily. Much of the material that I used I stumbled on purely by accident or by time-consuming search. A great deal more probably escaped me because it was hidden in other material, and since no one is oriented to think of interstate relations as a disparate subject, no one thought to look for material relating to them. It is time Australians recognized the existence and importance of the field. When they do, the student's job will be made vastly easier.

INDEX

Accident Insurance Office (Vic.): 92
Adelaide, S. A.: 27, 67, 100
Agricultural officers: 86
Agriculture: 30, 50, 153; Standing Committee on, 50-51. *See also* Primary production.
Air navigation: 134
Albury, N. S. W.: 100, 153
American Bar Association: 130
American Law Institute: 141
Apprenticeship: 60-61
Army, Commonwealth Minister for: 62
Art galleries: 97
Artesian basins: 158-59
Association of Government Printers of Australasia: 72, 75-76
Association of State Librarians of Australia: 73
Association of Superintendents of Insurance (Canada): 132
Attorney-General: 135, 137
Attorneys-General: 138; Standing Committee of, 142-51, 165
Australia and New Zealand City Transit Conference: 72, 75
Australia and New Zealand Railway Commissioners Conference: 72, 84
Australian Advisory Council on Bibliographical Services: 104
Australian Agricultural Council: 48-53, 54, 55, 67, 101
Australian Apprenticeship Advisory Committee: 48, 60-61
Australian Association for the Advancement of Science: 86
Australian Association of Psychiatrists: 85
Australian Barley Board: 101
Australian Capital Territory: *see* Canberra

Australian College of Education: 85
Australian College of Speech Therapists: 85
Australian Council for Educational Research: 85
Australian Dried Fruits Association: 86
Australian Dried Fruits Board: 101
Australian Education Council: 46
Australian Fisheries School: 55
Australian Labour Party: 3-4, 17, 167-69
Australian Loan Council: 41-43
Australian Medical Congress: 85
Australian Motor Vehicles Standards Committee: 64
Australian National Travel Association: 86
Australian National University: 8, 154, 155
Australian Port Authorities Association: 72, 78-80
Australian Road Research Board: 75
Australian Road Traffic Code Committee: 63-64
Australian Society of Neurologists: 85
Australian Teachers' Federation: 85
Australian Transport Advisory Council: 37, 48, 61, 62-65, 145
Australian Universities: Committee on, 156
Australian Water Fowl Council: 73
Australian Water Resources Council: 67-68, 159
Australian Wheat Board: 101

Barkly Basin: 158
Barwick, Garfield: 25-26, 137, 141
Barwon River: 125-27
Biennial Interstate Fauna Conference: 73, 84

ABOUT THE AUTHOR

Richard H. Leach has an extensive background of experience and study in the area of interstate relations. He has served on the staff of the Southern Regional Education Board, an interstate agency, and is the author of numerous articles on interstate relations in the United States and coauthor of a book on the subject, *The Administration of Interstate Compacts.* He has also published a study of interprovincial relations in Canada. Mr. Leach, who received the Ph.D. degree from Princeton University, is now an associate professor in the Department of Political Science at Duke University.

ABOUT THE BOOK

Interstate Relations in Australia was composed and printed by the Printing Department of the University of Kentucky. It is set in Linotype Electra, with ATF Bernhard Modern numerals for the chapter numbers. The title page is set in Klingspor Kumlien. The typographic design is by E. L. Taylor and Kenneth W. Elliott; the jacket artwork is by Mr. Taylor. The book is printed on Warren Olde Style antique wove stock and bound by the C. J. Krehbiel Company, Cincinnati, in Columbia Bayside Vellum cloth.